Going
PALEO
CW00458979

We're all part of something special and
I dedicate this book to *you*.

Nora and I invite you to share your beautiful,
light-filled energy and show the world what real
health and vitality look like.

Keep cooking with love and laughter for life and
remember, we are not extreme, merely informed,
and we thank you for joining the tribe!

PETE EVANS

with NORA GEDGAUDAS

Contents

FOREWORD *by Trevor Hendy*

If you are reading this book, you are probably considering 'going paleo'. The decision to embrace this way of life could be an incredible turning point in your life, and I want to talk about the power of making this kind of 'true' decision.

Photography by Brian Usher, *Ocean Road Magazine*

A true decision is all encompassing. It is one that implies your mind is already made up and you are non-negotiable about the outcome – flexible, perhaps, in the path you take to get there, but not willing to let it slip by. A true decision cuts through many levels to encompass soul, body and mind. To more fully understand the power of a decision you need to suspend the belief that we are just made up of mind and body and that we are only here to compete and survive as best we can. It's important to allow space for the possibility that your life is infused with a deeper meaning and that your very existence is not an accident but a graceful opportunity to express yourself and learn about yourself at a soul level.

I have been studying in the area of truth and wellness for 18 years and over this time have worked with many people at different stages of their journey. My online program, Bootcamp for the Soul, is designed to help people to go deeper and get in touch with their spirituality. This can require some hard work and honest self reflection, but life is not meant to be easy all of the time, otherwise there would be no growth, no learning, no realisations. In my work, I also spend a lot of time helping people to make true decisions, as I believe that what you do with your life and the opportunities that arise will be more within your control once you learn how to do this.

A vital step on the way to making a true decision is understanding that we attract whatever it is that we focus on most. There are so many different and powerful sayings that revolve around this idea:

What we focus on grows.
What we appreciate, appreciates.
Ask and you shall receive.
Build it and they will come.
If you think you can't then you are right, if you think you can, then you are also right.
If you can imagine it, you can achieve it.

One of the real wonders of working in my field is that I get to discover just how accurate these sayings are. I have a deep knowing that the world is our oyster and that we – each of us – are the pearls that are being created by the pressure of the world. As and when you are ready, you will no longer have to aim to just survive; you can begin to thrive. All you need to do is realise that you are a creator and that everything you need is actually already inside of you. Once you learn how to tune in to your soul, body and mind to make a true decision, you will have the ability to create the world and the life that you have always dreamed of for yourself. When you make that decision, the missing pieces can turn up.

When you don't make a decision, when you procrastinate, doubt, complain, whinge or justify why you can't do something, you also clearly send that impulse to every cell in your body, every layer of energy in your own sphere and out into the world. While making a decision can be very powerful, not making a decision can be equally so. It is like going to a restaurant and not bothering to place an order – you will surely be disappointed when nothing comes out and everyone else is eating.

Once you have made a decision, it's important to be patient and to not give up if things don't change immediately, or if it's more difficult than you imagined. If you did place that order at the restaurant, you wouldn't leave if it didn't come out in five minutes. You don't need to know how something is going to finish or even how it is going to start, you just need to know that you want to do it and begin by making the decision that you are going to do it – the rest will come. Your order will be delivered.

With a little more experience you will know that when you make a wholehearted decision, it is like placing an order for better conditions, for a more fulfilled and happier life. Eventually, you will know exactly what you want to order and who or what is capable of filling your order. Once you decide to make a positive change and pursue your best life, life itself will begin to deliver that order. Whether it is spiritual, mental and emotional freedom, better health, greater fitness, a beautiful relationship or some free time to pursue your passions, when you decide that you will start immediately, life will deliver what you need. All you have to do is be open to receiving it and willing to follow through.

So, in a nutshell, it's really just a matter of three simple steps. Once you have put these three things together, you have made a true decision and nothing will stop you.

1. Decide;
2. Be open to receiving;
3. Be willing to follow through.

And remember, you don't have to do it alone; if you allow it, life will be your greatest partner. Life will turn up in the form of inspirational people or moments and these will become part of your 'change team'. We have the knowledge between us to achieve our greatest dreams; you just have to put yourself in the best place to receive it. That starts with a decision, a true decision, one that you follow through with immediately. Bring it into now and never underestimate the power of who you are. Always think for yourself. If it is to be, it is up to you.

EAT
Tripe
FOR VIGOR
& STAMINA
CULTURE
FOR LIFE
pete evans

INTRODUCTION

Going paleo has transformed my life. And with the information and recipes in this book, I hope to help you transform your life as well – to become the healthiest and happiest version of yourself. The paleo way is not just a diet – it is a way of life that encompasses diet and food, sleep, relationships, exercise, respect for nature and overall wellbeing. It is a way of life that may just be the most powerful health approach for many of us.

I was 38 years old when I decided to go paleo. Until that point, I thought I was living a pretty healthy life by following our national guidelines for eating – the traditional food pyramid – which recommends a diet high in veggies, but also high in grains and with moderate amounts of legumes and dairy. Breakfast was muesli or wholegrain toast; lunch would be a wrap, a snag or some sushi; and at dinnertime the chef in me would come out and I would cook up a mean risotto or pasta, perhaps a curry with some rice, or a Moroccan tagine with couscous. Snacks throughout the day were bananas or muesli bars.

I honestly thought I was the healthiest chef around, but the thing was, I was constantly getting sick and I had terrible skin and digestive issues. My daughters were also having similar problems and I just couldn't work it out. I even wondered whether it was something in our genes. How wrong I was! What I did know for sure was that it was time for a change. I made the decision to not only examine my diet and lifestyle, but also to step away from every negative personal and business relationship that I was giving energy to, and to consciously invite positivity into my life.

Around this time, I crossed paths with a down-to-earth girl from New Zealand named Nic, who I'm now honoured to call my wife. Nic's knowledge-seeking spirit led us to a life-changing book called *Primal Body, Primal Mind* by bestselling American author and nutritional expert Nora Gedgaudas. I can remember Nic was sitting next to me reading it one night and I felt a sudden jab in my ribs. She had this look in her eye and I knew she had stumbled onto something powerful. She simply said: 'You need to read all of this.' Nora's book empowered us both with knowledge and inspired us to begin our own paleo journey, opening up a new life path for us, one that was laden with physical, mental and emotional health and clarity.

It was not always an easy transition. As I waded through the information in *Primal Body, Primal Mind* and other books, looking at the good and the bad aspects of various foods, I had to leave behind a lot of what I had been taught as a chef. I said goodbye to starchy carbs, refined sugar, toxic oils, dairy and legumes, and I said hello to a whole new world of nourishing alternatives. Initially I thought that I would have to completely abandon my extensive recipe repertoire, but then I realised that maybe I could find a way to turn 25 years of cooking experience into life-giving meals that could benefit people immensely. I immediately and excitedly embarked on a food adventure free of grains, dairy, legumes, refined sugar and toxic oils. In other words, I went paleo.

Going paleo has given me a life I could never have dreamt of. I have more energy now than I did as a kid and I can honestly say that I am in the best shape of my life. I wake up smiling and feeling refreshed, and have enough energy throughout the day to do anything that needs my attention:

making the kids a nutritious lunch, dedicating myself to various projects (and I have a few!) or spending quality time with my wife. My sleep has improved, as has my mental clarity, and the amount I want to achieve in this lifetime is staggering. I am not saying that I have all the answers, but what I do know is that going paleo has done wonders for me and for so many other people. I am honoured to share some of their personal stories here in these pages. Will we have new information to share and will this paleo way of living evolve? You bet. Research into gut microbes is in its infancy and I can guarantee that in years to come there will be a lot of new information on this and other areas of our health that will come to light. The fact that the paleo way is constantly growing and evolving as we learn more about our bodies through scientific research is something I find really exciting.

One of the most uplifting components of our paleo journey has been the response that we've received through social media and events. (I say 'we' because I'm joined on this real food pilgrimage by an amazing team of people, including my wife Nic, who are dedicated to sharing knowledge and encouraging people to make informed choices.) Through social media, we began to gain a new following. These people weren't exactly part of the foodie crowd; instead, they were people interested in the field of health or people suffering from a range of illnesses who were desperately seeking renewed health. Messages from grateful mothers, fathers, grandparents and people from all walks of life began to flood my inbox, with everyone sharing their own heartfelt stories of how going paleo had enabled them to reclaim their health or the health of their children and loved ones.

While I've never doubted that going paleo was the right decision for me, being part of this growing community who are enjoying the same awakened mental, emotional and physical health as my family and me has provided a form of support that I'm beyond grateful for! At the time of writing we have close to half a million followers and every day we post a story from somewhere in the world showing how the simple act of viewing food as medicine has changed peoples lives. There are stories from proud parents who have helped their children, grandparents who are now more active and healthy than they were 30 years ago, medical and health professionals who have witnessed incredible results, and many others. We now have a very strong tribe and we would love for you to join us.

Going Paleo is your complete practical guide to becoming part of the tribe and embracing this way of living that has helped so many people. The first half of the book is devoted to explaining the 'why' and 'how' of going paleo, while the second half of the book features some of my absolute favourite paleo recipes to help you get on your way. I am so proud to co-author the first section with Nora Gedgaudas, who has written the 'Why?' section, charting the latest research and science behind why our bodies perform best when we follow a diet similar to that of our ancestors. Nora has the most amazing scientific mind I have ever encountered and a heartfelt desire to help every single being on this planet. She doesn't sugar-coat things and she definitely won't recommend following an 80/20 rule (eating healthy foods 80 per cent of the time and unhealthy options 20 per cent of the time). We live in a society that strongly believes the old saying of 'everything in moderation', but if you look around, is this working out for us? How much diabetes, heart disease, autoimmunity or mental illness would you like to have in moderation? I am guessing the answer is none. There is an element of tough love to Nora's writing, but there is also an underlying gentle touch, and I hope her words trigger your hunger for even more information.

The 'How' section looks at all of the practicalities of embracing this lifestyle. There's a run-down on the foods and ingredients that have to go and what you can replace them with; a detailed guide to setting up your paleo kitchen; tips on everything from sticking with it to ways of incorporating more greens into your diet; and a kickstart eating plan to help you get started.

Finally, the recipes in this book reflect my avid love and respect for food. They are delicious, quick and affordable, specifically created to help busy people and families eat satisfying and nourishing food at every single meal. There are heaps of breakfasts, veggies and salads, main meals, snacks and drinks, and almost every recipe in the book can be made as a double or triple batch so that you always have healthy food in the fridge and are less likely to eat the foods you know you shouldn't. Cooking more than you need and enjoying the leftovers in different ways is absolutely key to making this lifestyle work, and once you get the hang of this style of cooking, I'm sure you'll love it as much as I do. I've also included a chapter for the basics – the bone broths, homemade sauces and dressings that play such an important role in the paleo lifestyle.

Going paleo has opened up a world of true health for me and my family. It has led me back to my roots, or rather my much-appreciated, pre-agriculture ancestors' roots. It has opened the doors wide to a glorious array of nutrient-dense ingredients that have enlivened me far more than any piece of bread or bowl of pasta ever did. I hope that this book will provide you with all the tools you'll need to fully embrace the paleo way, to start eating real, nutrient-dense food that will provide you with everything you need to look and feel your absolute best. So buckle up for some seriously exceptional, down-to-earth, honest information and recipes.

Cook with conscious love and be the shining example of who you are!

Pete x

Why

The SCIENCE BEHIND the PALEO WAY of EATING

by Nora Gedgaudas

The paleo way is an approach to eating that is in natural alignment with our prehistoric ancestral diet – the very one that forged our physiological make-up and our essential nutritional requirements. The time period we are talking about where we ate this way spans over 100,000 generations – not years, but 100,000 generations – of our evolutionary history: more than 3 million years.

In case the cynic in you or in your family is wondering … the answer is: No, this is not some fad diet. Let's just say that if this *were* a fad diet, then it would be the oldest fad diet in human history. In fact, it is more than a diet. Much more. The paleo way is an actual lifestyle that inspires you to make conscious choices about what you eat and how this impacts on your health and on the health of our planet. It is a way of life that inspires you to develop more of a direct relationship to your body and to where your food comes from. It inspires you to take responsibility for your own health in a positive, self-empowered way and to become a steward to your family's future, as well as a steward of the animals, plants and environment your food comes from. It is a way to restore your relationship with the cycle of life, of which we have always been a part but from which our species has, in more recent eras become blind to. It is coming home to our roots and foundations as a species and restoring our primal birthright: vibrant physical and mental health and a sustainable planetary future.

This is basic common sense.

Paleo as we are presenting it to you is an approach to eating that honours your body's most natural and essential nutritional requirements and avoids those things that we were never really designed to eat. Everything about it is rational and is supported by tens of thousands of research papers written in peer-reviewed journals over the last several decades – not just about the paleo way of living but the myriad subjects that surround and permeate this rich topic.

It embraces modern palaeoanthropology and human longevity science, helping us to better understand what constituted prehistoric human diets and what we have learned about humans living a long and disease-free life, so we can tweak these principles our ancestors followed to our best modern-day advantage. At the same time we need to take into account the uniquely challenging world in which we find ourselves today that our ancestors could never possibly have imagined.

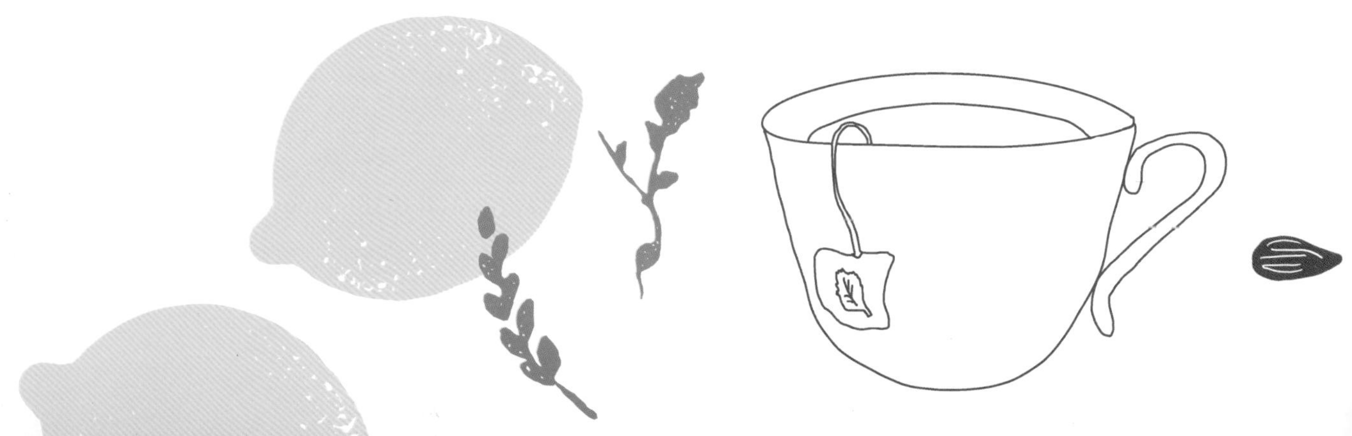

ONCE UPON A TIME ...

... there was no such thing as a food pyramid. There was no confusion about what did and did not constitute healthy eating. There were no such things as government guidelines, a food industry or a corporate agricultural monopoly and oil-based economy. There was also no such thing as obesity, metabolic disease, heart disease, cancer, diabetes, autoimmune disorders, Alzheimer's disease, chronic fatigue, ADD or widespread mental illness.

These are all modern-day inventions of our own making. By ignoring the principles that forged the make-up of our very being, we have compromised our own genome over the last few hundred generations, and especially over the last dozen or so.

In Australia one in two men and one in three women will have some form of cancer by the age of 85. And, shockingly, over 30 per cent of Australians suffer (knowingly) from one or more chronic diseases that are all potentially preventable by diet. It's a good bet that there isn't a single person reading this who doesn't have some symptom or health complaint or who doesn't at least know someone suffering from cancer, heart disease, diabetes, autoimmunity or some form of mental illness. My guess is that this is why you are reading this book.

Welcome to the modern world.

MY OWN STORY

I came to paleo by way of a rather convoluted path. Like many of you reading this, I spent the better part of my life believing that fat was bad and a carbohydrate-based diet was good – even necessary for my health. For a little while I was seduced by vegetarianism until the toll upon my health and wellbeing became too great for me to continue. During this time my existing tendency towards depression, anxiety and panic attacks utterly mushroomed – I even developed an eating disorder. At the time it did not occur to me that my diet was responsible for the way I was feeling. I was quite unaware of the devastating effects that grains, legumes and soy were having upon my immune system and therefore my entire body. Once I went back to eating animal source foods my negative symptoms subsided considerably. At the time it seemed counterintuitive, but now I totally understand why it made such a difference.

PARADIGM SHIFT

My passion for nutrition began in my mid-teens. Then I wanted to understand the minutiae of what specific nutrients did and what I could take to change the way I felt. I assumed most of the mainstream advice about diet was solid. My first real paradigm shift came in 1991 when I spent the summer living less than 800 kilometres from the North Pole with a family of wild wolves. I was in the company of world-renowned wolf biologist Dr L. David Mech, participating in some very exciting and unique behavioural research on wolves. But I digress …

Before leaving for my High Arctic polar sojourn my diet had been extremely high in plant foods with a little lean meat and fish thrown in. I assumed, while sitting on the frozen tundra, I would miss my garden-fresh diet, but when it came down to it nothing could have been further from the truth. Almost upon arrival on Ellesmere Island I began to fixate on fat-rich foods. I found myself craving butter, along with salami, cheese, red meat, nuts and nut butter. Not only was I eating a lot of fat but I was hardly moving. Given the mainstream mantra of low-fat eating and lots of exercise, one might have expected my body weight to balloon. In fact, the opposite happened. By the end of that summer I had lost roughly 11 kilograms of body fat. Needless to say, this got my attention. I filed it away in the back of my brain under: WTF?

During long hours of contemplation while I watched wolves sleep, which they did a lot that summer, I realised that humans had lived in this ancient and pristine land for more than 10,000 years without access to anything resembling fresh produce (save occasional berries found in certain parts of the Arctic and fermented vegetable matter from the stomachs of animals the native people hunted). How did humans live and thrive in this extreme climate without any meaningful access to plant foods?

The diet of the Inuit and ancient Thule cultures was almost purely carnivorous, with roughly 80 per cent of their caloric intake almost pure fat. In Resolute Bay, a small High Arctic outpost in the Queen Elizabeth Archipelago where I spent several days, the local Inuit people were still hunting and fishing as their ancestors had done and were eating a diet that was close to 80 per cent based on seals, whale blubber, musk ox, caribou, wild caught fish and other local fare. They seemed happy and healthy, as did the smiling and laughing children who played at all hours in the cold 24-hour sunlight, and no one I saw seemed obese.

CONNECTING THE DOTS

My Ellesmere adventure niggled at me for a few years, until one day I chanced upon a copy of Weston A. Price's classic and scholarly book *Nutrition and Physical Degeneration*. In it he chronicled the extraordinary health of native populations (including the Inuit) around the globe that were still eating traditional diets in the 1930s. One thing consistently revealed by his meticulous research – despite tremendous dietary and climatic variation among the groups – was the critical and even sacred importance of dietary fat and fat-soluble nutrients. Without exception, every healthy traditional population ate as many animal source foods and animal fats as were available to them. He found no vegan cultures anywhere in the world, even as he fervently searched for them. Of all the unique native groups Price studied, he found the Inuit to be among the healthiest mentally and physically, and among the most robust. Disease, mental health issues and nutritional deficiencies of any kind were exceedingly rare.

I finally got it. It was like being hit with a sack of wet cement. Upon my transition to a very low sugar and starch paleo way of eating, my health completely transformed. I knew I was onto something big. In the years that followed, as my research continued, I found myself refining my diet in ways that continued to improve my health. Dietary fat became increasingly central in its importance, while I eradicated all grains and legumes from my diet and increased my intake of fibrous vegetables and greens.

As a long-time member of the Life Extension Foundation, to me the logical place to go to find scientific answers was the realm of human longevity research, which seeks to determine what foods help us live the longest. I looked at essential elements from ancestral diets and applied longevity research principles, combining the best of both ancient and modern perspectives.

I also found I was far from alone. I came across dozens of cutting-edge thinkers, mentors, medical experts and researchers who had arrived at some or many of the same conclusions I had. The strength for me was in seeing how these concepts were interrelated and I proceeded to connect the dots into a more cohesive picture.

The paleo way isn't about treating disease but instead systematically restoring the conditions essential for optimal health. Given the appropriate raw materials, your body's capacity for self-healing is enormous. Our aim with this book is to give you an alternative to the mainstream Western diet that you can implement and afford. We make no medical claims to cure or prevent diseases, but we offer a paradigm that can support your best possible health and wellbeing. I am deeply honoured to be a part of sharing something that can help others with true self-empowerment and unstoppable health.

WELCOME TO THE 21ST CENTURY

The image of someone sitting on a couch and watching football on TV while eating chips and a triple-cheese stuffed-crust pizza and washing it down with a beer is light years away from any image of someone wearing animal furs while holding a spear and stalking giant aurochs in Ice Age Europe.

As a species, we have managed to isolate ourselves from the very environment that surrounds and sustains us. We live today in artificial, climate-controlled environments and bask in the new 24-hour daylight we have created for ourselves through the invention of electricity and light bulbs. We communicate with our family members and friends through sound bites on compact electronic devices (sometimes even while in the same house or sitting at the same table). We have grown largely indifferent to changes of the seasons around us, to the weather, to all the telltale subtleties of sights, sounds and smells of the forest – numb to our instincts – and numb even to our communal sense of family and tribe.

We buy our food in cardboard boxes or in shrink-wrapped packages with labels on them that most people don't bother to read. The modern day forest where we hunt and forage for the food that is meant to sustain us is found within the walls of a sterile building filled with rows and rows of substances no prehistoric ancestor would even begin to recognise as food. And it requires no more skill to obtain any of it than swiping a card over an electronic reading device. Boom. Dinner. We think nothing of the animals, fowl or fish, whose lives were sacrificed for our meals, or the conditions in which they spent their often meaningless, cruel and tortured existences. There is nothing sacred in this act of animal/plant sacrifice or in eating. We no longer have any first-hand knowledge of where our food actually comes from, and most people shopping for it couldn't care less. It's too inconvenient to care.

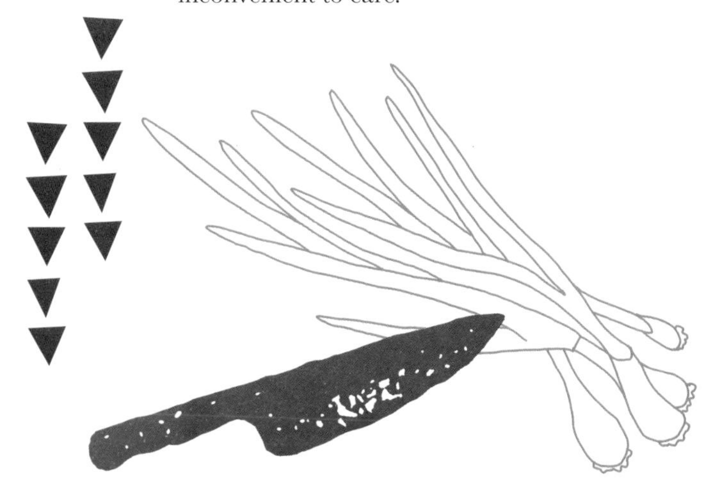

Most people in our modern society seem to be incapable of surviving a day without access to electricity and a nearby convenience store. As a species we have never been more vulnerable or weak. Exercise for many of us consists of walking from the closest parking spot we can find to the front door of a fast food restaurant. In short, we've lost our natural way.

Why should this matter to us? Because 99.99 per cent of all our genes were formed before the advent of agriculture and 100 per cent of them before the advent of our industrialised food supply. In spite of our modern day surroundings, we are still genetically identical to those who came before us in prehistoric, pre-agricultural times. And we have the exact same nutritional requirements they did. We are physiologically and genetically every bit still them – just a weaker version in need of remembering what they once knew.

THE AUSTRALIAN DIET

According to an Australian Health Survey recently published by the Australian Bureau of Statistics:

- 95% of Australians eat bread and cereal products;
- 85% consume milk and other dairy products;
- 69% get about 14% of total caloric energy intake from meat, mostly chicken (factory farmed and grain-fed);
- 75% consume vegetables but 25% consider potatoes (pure starch) as vegetables;
- 60% eat fruit and 'fruit dishes' (whatever that means);
- 35% eat processed snack foods with no nutritional value (this is probably under reported);
- Most calories come from carbohydrate-based foods.

Is it any wonder many of us today are fat, sick and physically or mentally unhealthy? We no longer live in alignment with our natural blueprint. We need to get over the illusion that our modern day state of human evolution is superior to those so-called 'primitive' ancestors who preceded us. We're not even close to being as physically robust. Heck, our brains are even smaller.[1]

We are all, whether we know it or not – or even like it or not – very much genetically still Palaeolithic beings. Our bodies have the same need for the same kind of food that forged our physiological make-up and basic nutritional requirements. The further we stray from this awareness, the further we stray from optimal physical and mental health. Understanding this is the first step towards reclaiming our true primal birthright: a healthy, lean body and an optimally functioning brain.[2] It should not be too much to ask.

SO WHAT EXACTLY IS A PALEO WAY OF EATING?

This can be a complicated question to answer since our Palaeolithic history goes back almost 3 million years and involves an enormous range of foods that span a variety of early human habitats and seasonal and climatic conditions. Humans have occupied every ecological niche upon planet earth and have made use of hundreds of species of animals, plants, insects, seafood and other aquatic foods. All this may sound hopelessly complicated and confusing until you realise that certain basic and rather simple dietary principles were consistent, regardless of habitat, season or climate. In short, we were always hunter-gatherers living off the land for the bulk of our calories and nutrition. In other words, we got most of our nutrition from good-quality unadulterated proteins and fats and supplemented them with plant foods.

Also, despite the fact that it is difficult to nail down with precision everything we might have eaten along the way, it is important to point out that there were certain foods we know with a fair degree of certainty weren't eaten and could not in any way be essential to us now.

Before I continue I want to touch upon the concept of bio-individuality – the popular notion that we are all different. Although there is some truth to this idea and it sounds rather appealingly rational, it is given far too much weight. As humans, physiologically we are far more alike than we are unalike. We all require a similar range of protein, fats and other macronutrients and micronutrients in order to have what we need to function well. We all share a blood pH of between 7.35 and 7.45. We all have fat-based brains and nervous systems. We all more or less (with some gender-based variations) have the same organs, hormones, neurotransmitters and glands and we all experience some adverse physiologic effects from glycaemic foods to one degree or another. Although there may be a range of tolerances for certain things, some of this is symptomatic of deeper problems that may need to be addressed. Food sensitivities are a modern day phenomenon that have a lot to do with incorporating new kinds of foods into our diets in the last few thousand years – and even the last few decades – that we were never designed to eat. Grains, legumes and dairy products come to mind as being among the most common dietary antigens generating immune reactivity and systemic and/or gastrointestinal inflammation.

We know from the stable isotopic analysis of human bone collagen that has been extensively researched through the Max Planck Institute for Evolutionary Anthropology in Leipzig, Germany, that although occasional consumption of wild cereal grasses may have occurred, there is no evidence to suggest that they were ever a significant part of our diet prior to the development of agriculture.[3,4,5,6,7]

We also know that evolving humans had very limited access to and limited capacity to digest sugars and starches. In their raw form, starchy tubers are quite indigestible and would have required extensive heating to liberate the starch molecules (a process known as gelatinisation) to allow them to be eaten. Even if we ever did that to any significant extent, these foods would have:

1. presented varying and often significant degrees of toxicity
2. yielded a mere fraction of the energy and nutrient value that meat and animal fat can readily provide – especially for our energy-intensive, fat-dependent brains.

The evidence overwhelmingly seems to suggest that for the last 2 million years we relied upon a primarily hunting economy, eating large land-based mammals, which we supplemented with fish, fowl, reptiles, insects, nuts, a few eggs and some limited small, tart, fibrous fruit and berries; together with whatever above-ground, non-toxic fibrous plants and herbs were available.

HOW CAN IT BE POSSIBLE TO EAT A PALAEOLITHIC DIET TODAY?

The answer is simple: we rely upon the basic principles associated with their diet. In other words, to mimic the diet that we were designed to consume, all we need to do is select from the food groups our Palaeolithic ancestors recognised: meat, fish and fowl that are fed as naturally as possible, a big variety of organically grown fibrous plants and herbs, plus as much dietary fat from a diverse range of natural sources as might be needed to satisfy the appetite. Nuts (preferably activated to help neutralise antinutrients and maximise their digestibility) and berries may be enjoyed occasionally, with fruit used mainly as a periodic treat, rather than a daily indulgence.

It is important to understand that no dietary sugar is our friend – and of all the sugars, fructose (the one primarily found in fruit and fruit juices) is far and away the least friendly to our health and longevity. Honey also contains appreciable amounts of fructose. Even plain glucose does some damage (through a process called glycation) and can cause metabolic dysregulation. And all starch becomes sugar once it is digested and hits your blood stream.

ONE SOURCE OF POSSIBLE CONFUSION

The paleo approach to eating was the single most Googled diet in 2013.[8] As the popularity has grown, so have the number of versions. It has become quite a circus: with everything from supposedly paleo-friendly processed foods and snacks to desserts, cocktails, protein powders and convoluted modifications of Palaeolithic principles catering to modern tastes, cravings, wishful thinking, biases and political agendas.

Still, for other people embracing this movement, paleo is less about eating what our ancestors ate and more about avoiding what they didn't eat (grains, sugars, processed foods, pasteurised dairy, industrial seed oils and legumes – especially soy).

This book looks more comprehensively at both sides of this coin – what our ancestors did and didn't eat. But it also looks at this in the context of the world we live in today and how we might optimise this approach to meet modern needs and challenges.

Finally, there is a fair and legitimate question that in my view needs to be addressed:

JUST BECAUSE OUR ANCESTORS ATE SOMETHING, IS THAT A GOOD ENOUGH REASON FOR US TO EAT THE SAME THING NOW?

As opportunistic omnivores we would have done and eaten whatever we needed to do to survive. Does this make a food healthy, beneficial or even okay for us simply because our ancestors ate it or because we survived as a species in spite of it?

This question is one I asked myself many years ago. After all, we are living in a very different world today fraught with modern perils that would have been inconceivable to our ancestors. What was tolerable to them might not be tolerable to us today. We also have the unique modern day advantage of science we can use to delve into how our bodies respond to various foods and nutrients. This can shed a unique light on the subject that can help us optimise underlying Palaeolithic principles.

For instance, does the fact that our distant ancestors ate enormous amounts of meat every chance they got mean that we need to do the same thing now, or that we somehow should? Not at all – in fact, human longevity research and basic human physiology suggest that although it is very important that we get our protein from complete sources, such as animal source foods, there is no modern advantage to exceeding the amount that our body requires for its maintenance and repair in a given day – in fact, there may even be longer term detriments to our health.

Just because we were capable of putting a particular food in our mouths and surviving doesn't mean we thrived or that our health was enhanced. Cases in point: grains, legumes, starches and sugars. Even though we did occasionally eat these, it turns out that their inclusion in our diet always represents a form of compromise to our physiological and immunological make-up. In short, it is abundantly clear from palaeoanthropologic and immunologic research that we are not designed to be at our best on a diet containing grains and legumes. Our ancestors may have gotten away with a few of these things in relative health, but they weren't exposed to anywhere near as much compromise as we are today. We have far less wiggle room for error or indulgence.

In fact, when it comes to grains, according to world famous researcher and expert on the impact of grains on human health Dr Alessio Fasano, no human being anywhere on the planet is capable of even digesting (much less healthfully utilising) the protein in grains.[9] We also know that grains and legumes contain numerous compounds that are highly detrimental to our bodies and brains (i.e. lectins, phytates, trypsin inhibitors, goitrogens, excitotoxins, etc.) many of which cannot be neutralised through cooking.

It's important to point out that, of the three major macronutrients, protein, fat and carbohydrates, the only one for which there is no recognised or established human dietary requirement in any medical or physiology textbook anywhere is carbohydrates. Although the human body does require a small amount of glucose for its day-to-day functioning – and in an emergency – all we ever need can be readily supplied through two basic internal processes: gluconeogenesis (the process through which glucose is manufactured from proteins and fats) and glycogenolysis (the breakdown of stored/surplus carbohydrate in the form of glycogen found in your liver and muscle tissue). This said, it is nearly impossible to eat a zero carb diet and the small amounts present in green fibrous vegetables are more than sufficient to meet or exceed any daily foundational requirements, especially if you are well adapted to relying on fat as your primary source of fuel.

> 'It is possible to suffer an amino acid deficiency. It is possible to have an essential fatty acid deficiency. But there is no such thing as a carbohydrate deficiency.'
>
> *Dr Richard K Bernstein* Fellow of the American College of Nutrition, the American College of Endocrinology and The College of Certified Wound Specialists

The primary source of energy humans are best designed to rely on is fat (ketones, the energy units of fat, and free fatty acids) – your body's and brain's super fuel. Fat contains more than double the calories per gram of carbohydrates, is far more efficiently stored and can be readily drawn upon, evenly burned and effortlessly relied upon for energy for extended periods of time, even in the absence of regular meals. When your body is accustomed to burning fat (and not sugar) as its primary source of fuel you are hungry less frequently, have far fewer, if any, cravings, have much more reliable energy throughout the day, have stabilised moods and better cognitive function, less inflammation and increased blood flow to your brain – up to 39 per cent more.[10]

Relying on fat as your primary source of fuel is the most natural state for you to be in. It also provides an enormous variety of health benefits, including effortless weight loss, improved mood, memory, brain function, heart health, endocrine function (i.e. hormonal health) and the potential to stave off diseases, such as cancer, diabetes, autoimmunity and Alzheimer's disease among many, many others. What's not to love about that?

BUT DOESN'T FAT MAKE YOU FAT?

In short, No. By itself, dietary fat will absolutely not make you fat.[11] You are only likely to store dietary fat when it is eaten with sugar and starch. Your body will always try to burn the sugar first, and it is impossible to burn fat at the same time you are producing insulin (in response to the sugar and starch). In the presence of insulin your body will typically store the fat for later. In the absence of sugar and starch, quality dietary fat supplies:

- more efficiently produced aerobic adenosine triphosphate (ATP) energy;
- primary structure to your brain and nervous system;
- a substrate for hormone and neurotransmitter production, as well as their receptors;
- a plethora of fat-soluble nutrients needed for gene transcription and healthy gene expression.

'Recent studies have shown that D-beta-hydroxybutyrate, the principal "ketone", is not just a fuel, but a "superfuel" more efficiently producing ATP energy than glucose or fatty acid.'[12]

Only once these structural and functional needs are met within your body do excesses of dietary fat potentially become available for fat storage. The fact is, though, that dietary fat by itself is very satisfying to the appetite and is difficult to overeat. Most dietary sugars (and all starches are sugar once they are digested and hit your bloodstream), on the other hand, in excess of what you need for immediate emergency energy, are invariably converted to triglycerides in your liver and then stored as body fat (once your glycogen reserves get topped off, which happens quickly). It's not natural dietary fat that makes us gain weight and damages our hearts (and everything else), dietary sugars and starches are the culprits – particularly the refined varieties found in processed foods and high-fructose sweeteners.[13,14]

After years of trying – and failing – to lose weight with the calories in/calories out method, I started following a strict elimination diet three and a half years ago. Since then, I have lost 23 kg. It has been trial and error but with the re-introduction of foods I, reluctantly at first, have accepted that my body does best grain free and sugar free. It's also clear that the nutritional advice we've been following is not working for many people. I've loved learning a whole new approach to eating and I'm reaping the benefits. I feel like myself again, suffer from fewer and less intense migraines, have much more stamina and all the aches and pains that I thought I had to accept as part of ageing have gone!

Anthea, 46 years

WHAT CHANGES WILL GOING PALEO BRING ABOUT?

Among the first positive things you will notice is an overall improved sense of wellbeing, more prolonged energy and some fairly rapid reductions in excess weight. Mind you, you should not be thinking of this way of eating as some sort of short-term weight-loss diet. The whole point to this approach lies in the overall improvement of your health, wellbeing and functioning, which tends to also include healthy weight loss (or weight normalisation) as a natural consequence. Health is always your first priority.

Usually pretty early into the transition from being a sugar burner to a fat burner, many people feel almost immediate relief from aches and pains, chronic inflammation, mood swings, poor sleep, trouble focusing and chronic fatigue.

You may find yourself becoming evangelical about the changes you're experiencing; rather than getting on a soapbox, it's better to focus on your transformation. Ghandi is commonly quoted as saying in relation to this: 'Be the change you want to see in the world.' What Ghandi actually said was: 'If we could change ourselves, the tendencies in the world would also change. As a man changes his own nature, so does the attitude of the world change towards him … We need not wait to see what others do.' Both points of wisdom apply here. Eventually, you'll set an example of what going paleo can do and people start asking how you did it. There is nothing more convincing than a robust example.

Keep in mind, too, that even with the best possible change can come temporary discomfort as your body adjusts to an entirely new state of metabolic functioning. The transition period of shifting from being a sugar burner to a fat burner takes a good three to six weeks in my experience. The fullest extent of ketogenic adaptation is typically established within two to three months.

The interim can be a little bumpy for a few people, depending on where they are when they start on this path to better health. Some people may experience detoxification symptoms (minor headaches, flu-like symptoms and temporary fatigue or malaise). This is why hydration is so important. Mind you, since dietary sugar and starch cause your body to retain a lot of excess extracellular water weight (the kind that makes you look puffy), once they are removed from your diet you will let go of these undesirable excesses quickly, which frequently shows as rapid initial weight loss. Do not let anyone tell you that this is the only source of your weight loss when it comes to this way of eating. It isn't true. It is perfectly normal, natural and even desirable. On the other side of this will come a healthier normalisation of your body composition – which should be anyone's ultimate goal. In other words, what happens on the bathroom scale isn't as important as what is happening with retaining your lean tissue mass (which weighs more than fat) and how much excess fat loss is occurring.

The fact that your body more readily releases excess fluids and sodium in the beginning simply speaks of the need for good hydration. Excess protein can also result in rapid fluid loss but the approach to paleo eating we present here is not a high protein diet. Moderating your protein intake and relying on fat as your primary source of fuel ultimately results in healthy weight loss of excess body fat, while retaining your lean tissue mass (i.e. muscle). Protein moderation is more likely to support your better overall health and longevity and help your body to maintain its dependence on fat as a primary source of fuel. It is also more affordable and sustainable for your wallet and the planet.

Moderating your protein intake and relying on fat as your primary source of fuel ultimately results in healthy weight loss of excess body fat.

If you experience a little constipation during your transition, this usually has to do with your body losing sodium. By using full-spectrum healthy sources of salt, such as Himalayan sea salt, you can easily restore your sodium balance and these constipation issues will typically go away. You'll be getting plenty of fibre from the vegetables and greens you are eating, so this is not a fibre-related issue.

If you are normally prone to blood-sugar issues, you may experience a few more of those symptoms during the transition as your body learns how to shift to a different primary source of fuel. In the short term, you might benefit from a more gradual approach, starting with a little snacking on small amounts of nuts or other protein/fat-rich foods between meals. Certain supplements like L-glutamine powder (best used under the tongue) can also be helpful in minimising these symptoms and associated cravings for some.

Many people find that they are able to take the plunge and do it all at once and it works out fine. It's just a matter of taking the necessary steps and seeing how you feel, then adjusting your approach as you need to. You will get there!

WHAT CAN GOING PALEO HELP WITH?

It is important to repeat that we are not promoting any sort of treatment here for any specific illness or medically related issue. We aren't claiming that this approach will prevent any possibility of disease. That said, improving your overall health and giving your body better raw materials with which to build it, tends to improve symptoms you may be prone to.

In my private practice as a nutritionist, I have witnessed and/or received innumerable reports of improvement in the areas below:

- mood stabilisation
- reduced/eliminated depression
- reduced/eliminated anxiety
- improved cognitive functioning
- enhanced and evened-out energy levels
- cessation of seizures
- improved overall neurological stability
- cessation of migraines
- improved sleep
- dramatic improvement in autistic symptoms
- improvements with polycystic ovarian syndrome
- improved GI (glycaemic index) functioning
- healthy weight loss
- cancer remissions/tumour shrinkage
- much better management of underlying previous health issues
- improved symptoms and quality of life in those struggling with various forms of autoimmunity (including many with type 1 and 1.5 diabetes)
- reversal of type 2 diabetes
- diminishment and/or total disappearance of arthritic symptoms
- fewer colds and flus
- total reversal of chronic fatigue
- improved memory
- sharpened cognitive functioning
- significantly stabilised temperament.

My family's paleo journey started just over two years ago when my 4-year-old son became extremely ill with Crohn's disease. We left the hospital with a ton of medication and instructions to put him on a six-week formula diet and to let him eat anything he wanted. After the six weeks on formula, we reintroduced food and within four weeks he was heading towards a relapse. I could not accept that this was going to be my son's life forever, so I did some research and decided to start our family on a paleo way of eating. That was two years ago now and he's just had a colonoscopy/endoscopy that showed no visible Crohn's and biopsies that confirm there is zero inflammation. The medication that the doctors had told me would be for life and which could potentially give him cancer are gone. My son is strong and healthy, our family is much healthier and my 2-year-old daughter knows no other way of eating.

Penny, 37 years

AVOIDING PROCESSED FOODS

The first major assault to the health of humans, not to mention to our planet, was the agricultural revolution, roughly 10,000 years ago. The reliance on grains and legumes led to a fairly immediate and significant deterioration of human health. We lost stature, bone density, lean tissue mass, brain size and half our life expectancy. Yes, you heard correctly: our Palaeolithic ancestors actually lived longer and substantially healthier lives than our more recent ancestors who adopted an agricultural lifestyle.

The significant consumption of grains and legumes that accompanied this radical Neolithic revolution has occupied less than a heartbeat in human evolution: only about 0.4 per cent of our entire evolutionary history. Since that time, we have genetically changed a mere 0.005 per cent and have yet to fully adapt to this newer way of life. Now 10,000 years may sound like a long time, but in evolutionary terms it is virtually negligible. Less than 500 generations have transpired since the early human implementation of an agricultural lifestyle and, if anything, we are actually becoming less adapted to these foods. In one large and important study published in 2009 in the peer-reviewed journal *Gastroenterology* the researchers tested 10,000 available blood samples that had been carefully stored in a military hospital from 50 years ago and compared them to 10,000 blood samples from people today. They discovered that there has been a 400 per cent increase in the incidence of coeliac disease within the last 50 years, alone! This conclusion had absolutely nothing to do with improvements in modern day testing versus testing accuracy from 50 years ago, as all available samples were in fact tested using the same modern methods. The implications for these foods upon our health aren't good.

But agriculture alone was not the only major post-Palaeolithic compromise to human health. About 250 years ago we underwent the Industrial Revolution; the refinement and more profitable mass production of pre-packaged foods and food-like substances began to take place. Since then, the radical acceleration of the diseases of modern civilisation have followed an exponential curve in a deadly direction.

One particular case involves the development of what we now recognise as cardiovascular disease. A medical student graduating from university in 1910 had never even heard of this condition. But in 1911, the first four documented cases of a rare new condition called coronary thrombosis were published in the *Journal of the American Medical Association*. A doctor by the name of Paul Dudley White became fascinated with this unusual new disease. When he elected to pursue it as a primary course of interest, his colleagues thought he was mad and mostly wasting his time. By the 1950s, however, cardiovascular disease was recognised as a leading cause of death among those living in the modern industrialised world. Is this because we suddenly started eating red meat and cholesterol? Of course not. But by this time, there was a great deal of money to be made from processed foods. Pointing the finger where it belonged, which Dr White attempted to do, was met with considerable and aggressive resistance by industry and others profiting from this message. Blaming meat and naturally occurring fat/cholesterol for the problems we were seeing, allowed industry and well-funded government agencies to capitalise on the illusion – an illusion that persists to this very day.

Interestingly, the rates of virtually all forms of disease, particularly cancer, heart disease, metabolic disorder (i.e., type 2 diabetes, obesity, etc.) and autoimmunity, have continued to rise in the face of increased grain, carbohydrate and processed vegetable oil consumption, despite a statistically significant drop in the consumption of animal fat and dietary cholesterol. Yet dietary animal fat and cholesterol continue to be blamed.

'The diet-heart hypothesis (that suggests that high intake of fat and cholesterol causes heart disease) has been repeatedly shown to be wrong, and yet, for complicated reasons of pride, profit and prejudice, the hypothesis continues to be exploited by scientists, fund-raising enterprises, food companies, and even governmental agencies. The public is being deceived by the greatest health scam of the century.'

Dr George V Mann, Formerly with the Framingham Heart Study Project

MINIMISING SUGAR

What's so bad about carbohydrates, anyway? Don't we actually need to eat them? The answer to the last question is an emphatic: No. We were never designed to eat dietary sugars and starch as a significant part of our diet. In Palaeolithic times our access to them was limited. When we consume them our bodies undergo a variety of unhealthy compromises.

By itself sugar has an inherently damaging effect on our tissues and generates something called glycation. Glycation, a process by which sugars combine with proteins and fats in our bodies and causes them to malfunction, is responsible for ageing and leads to deterioration of our joints, our organ function, our immune system and, most dangerous of all, our brains. In fact, the human brain may be the single most vulnerable tissue to glycation of any in the body. Our brain, made up of delicate fats and responding poorly to insulin, becomes a target for inflammation and neurodegeneration in the presence of even slightly elevated glucose levels. According to the authors in two recently published studies, 'Higher fasting serum glucose levels in cognitively normal, non-diabetic adults may be associated with Alzheimer's disease pathophysiology.'[15] And: 'Our results suggest that higher glucose levels may be a risk factor for dementia, even among persons without diabetes.'[16]

Alzheimer's disease is now being classified as type 3 diabetes in recognition of sugar's harmful impact on the health of the human brain. A dietary fat-based metabolic approach, such as the one presented in this book, has been demonstrated to help prevent and even reverse the ravages and symptoms of Alzheimer's disease and other forms of dementia.

The action of glycation on your body's cells and tissues also attracts what is called free radical activity, basically, inflammation, adding further compromise to an already bad situation. Incorporating a dietary fat-based approach while eliminating sugar and starch, on the other hand, helps reduce free radical activity and improves antioxidant activity, while also improving your brain's and body's utilisation of oxygen and supplying it with a more reliable source of energy. There is no downside to your long-term health if this is done properly, as is frequently emphasised in the published research.

With respect to metabolic needs in the human body, our brain is our most expensive organ. It occupies only 5 per cent or less of our total mass, but it utilises at least 20 per cent or more of our body's energy supply to meet its considerable demands. Fat provides more calories per gram on average than any available energy source. It is what the human brain in particular hungers for. The brain can and does use glucose, especially when a person consumes a diet that is dominated by carbohydrates or during an emergency, though glucose isn't as essential to the day-to-day functioning of the brain as is commonly believed. In fact, ketones – those energy units of fat – are an abundant, stable and steady source of fuel, even in the absence of regular meals. They don't require constant replenishing. All of us – even if we're slender – have plenty of fat to burn once we've conditioned ourselves to make the best use of it. It's also the human body's most natural primary energy source. But the only way to get good at burning fat (as with anything) is by doing more of it.

The habitual inclusion of dietary sugar and starch stimulates the regular release of your body's fat-storage hormone, insulin. Insulin was originally meant to take excess nutrients in our diet and move them into storage in case of a future famine. We ate more ripe fruit in the late summer and autumn months as a way of fattening ourselves up (just like bears do) for the long winter ahead – only nowadays winter doesn't come anymore. We all live in comfortable climate-controlled environments. Periodic insulin resistance isn't something that offers us any sort of advantage anymore – it's a massive health liability.

It just so happens, though, that virtually every molecule of sugar or starch we eat is considered excess to our metabolism and chronic insulin production has been associated with everything from obesity and cardiovascular disease to cancer and significantly reduced life expectancy. Insulin also attracts inflammation and tends to elevate cortisol levels, which further elevates your blood sugar. It becomes a vicious cycle that can eventually develop into what is called metabolic disorder (formerly called Syndrome X). Metabolic disorder includes obesity, diabetes, cardiovascular disease, PCOS (polycystic ovarian syndrome), low testosterone in men and depressed oestrogen in women, depressed immune function and inflammatory processes.

The second most common thing to stimulate insulin production is excess dietary protein. Interestingly, a significant percentage of excess dietary protein is actually converted to sugar and may be used the same way. The more dependent you are on sugar as a primary source of fuel, the more your body will convert its protein stores into sugar to meet the constant demand. Keep in mind that your muscle tissue, including your heart, and your bones are a significant source of protein that may be drawn from for this purpose.

The field of human longevity research took a quantum leap forward in the last decade when it unexpectedly came to recognise insulin's central role in premature ageing and death.[17] The same approach to diet discussed in this book was found in a 2009 research study to improve several biomarkers of ageing.[18] It turns out that the less insulin we need in the course of our lifetimes the longer we are likely to live and the healthier we are likely to be. Similarly, low leptin levels, blood sugar, triglycerides and even T3 thyroid hormones have shown consistently as healthy biomarkers of ageing. Seeing as dietary sugar and starch are the primary means through which excess insulin is generated, and as there is no established dietary requirement for these foods whatsoever, to me it becomes a no-brainer. By mostly eliminating dietary sugar and starch you effectively remove a major compromise to every aspect of your physical, mental and cognitive health and potentially add meaningfully to your own life expectancy and quality of life.

PALEO KEEPS YOU FEELING FULL FOR LONGER

Anyone eating a carbohydrate-based diet with a significant amount of sugars and starches (100 grams a day or more) is relying on sugar as their primary metabolic source of fuel. Why might this be less than desirable?

FIRING UP YOUR METABOLIC WOOD STOVE

Think of your metabolism as running like a wood stove. If you need to heat your home all the time using this wood stove, what type of fuel would do the most effective and efficient job?

Carbohydrates are the metabolic equivalent of using kindling to fuel your metabolic fire. Complex carbohydrates, such as whole grains, beans, brown rice, sweet potatoes, etc. are somewhat akin to putting twigs on that fire. Refined grains, bread, pasta, white rice, potatoes and the like are

the metabolic equivalent of putting crumpled up paper on that fire. Alcohol, fruit juices and sugary beverages and sports drinks are much like squirting on lighter fluid.

If you had to heat your house using mainly kindling, you could certainly do it but with what result? You would be preoccupied with where the next handful of fuel is coming from to keep the fire going. If you go too long without feeding the fire, the house starts to get cold and you start packing more fuel (and maybe even a little lighter fluid) into the wood stove. You are conditioning yourself to crave that kind of fuel all day long and you effectively become a slave to your metabolic woodstove.

But what is the alternative?

Why not reach for a nice big *fat* log to put on that fire? Voila! All of a sudden you're free. The log will burn for a long time before you need to add another one. You can go about your business and not worry about the fire going out.

Fat is our ultimate metabolic fuel. Ketones are a superfuel producing energy even more efficiently than glucose or free fatty acids. Your brain absolutely loves ketones, and by relying on fat as a primary source of fuel you can improve the blood flow to your brain, your memory and cognitive performance, your mental energy, clarity and your moods.

Understand that ketone body metabolism is a state in which you utilise fat and not sugar for your primary source of fuel. It is a state cultivated through a process called ketogenic adaptation, which involves carbohydrate restriction and the predominant inclusion of calories from fat. Research shows that: 'The effects of ketone body metabolism suggest that ketosis may offer therapeutic potential in a variety of different common and rare disease states.'[19]

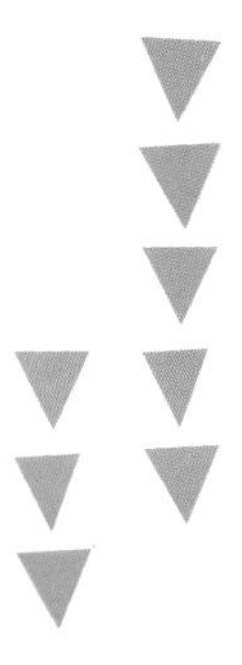

Relying on sugar is like living your metabolic life on a roller coaster (and not the fun kind). Your body is obsessed with maintaining the lowest level of blood sugar needed at any given time, so if you are dependent on sugar as your main fuel you need to replenish it much more often. Fat, however, is a nutrient-dense food that is more satisfying and nourishing than those comparatively nutrient-poor sugary or starchy carbohydrates. By relying on fat as your primary source of fuel, you will feel full for longer and find yourself eating fewer calories.

By the way, although fibrous vegetables and greens are also technically carbohydrates, they have a very low amount of sugar or starch in them. And because plant foods contain numerous beneficial compounds (phytonutrients and antioxidants) that help us detoxify and combat environmental pollutants and other toxic compounds, there is really no restriction on how much of this type of carbohydrate you can eat.

YOUR BODY'S MOST IMPORTANT HORMONE

Another reason you will feel less hungry eating the paleo way is that the human body produces an extremely important hormone, called leptin. In fact, it may just be the most important hormone you have. Leptin was discovered relatively recently in a place they did not expect to find it: inside our fat cells. Prior to this everyone thought that body fat was just an ugly form of excess stored energy. Now we know that fat cells are actually a very sophisticated endocrine organ, producing a number of compounds we need in order to survive, though, when produced in excess, can generate chronic inflammation. Leptin, the most important of these compounds, is your body's own internal fat sensor. Dietary fat speaks the language leptin knows best. Sugars and starch 'scream' at leptin and cause it to become dysregulated or resistant (just like insulin resistance) and confused. In a way, leptin and insulin are birds of a feather: consumption of excess dietary carbohydrate leads to their dysregulation. Leptin, though, is king.[20] 'Leptin is involved in the hormonal regulation of the reproductive, somatotropic, thyroid, and autonomic axes and ultimately in the regulation of energy balance.'[21]

Wow, that's a lot of responsibility for one little hormone!

As fundamentally Ice Age beings, fat to our bodies means survival; and survival trumps everything else. If you don't get enough fat, your body panics and thinks you're somehow starving. You may find yourself craving sugar and starch, which your body stores as excess body fat. Your body also starts to produce unhealthy leptin and insulin surges in response to rushes of blood sugar from all the carbs, and this ends up making you hungrier and wanting to eat more. At the same time, your body becomes extremely efficient at storing fat and hangs on to it like a pit bull.

Get the picture?

DID YOU KNOW?

For healthier weight and body composition, a healthier brain and immune system and mood stabilisation, a fat-based metabolism wins every time. Keeping your blood sugar, insulin and leptin levels low are among the most reliable markers of longevity there are.

If, on the other hand, you supply your body with enough fat (in the absence of sugar and starch) to quietly satisfy your appetite and calm leptin, then you are sending a message to leptin that 'hunting is good'. Your body doesn't have to hoard the cumbersome stores of fat and will burn it more naturally and freely. This is why eating fat does not make you fat and, in fact, helps people lose weight efficiently. The scientific evidence is in. For healthier weight and body composition, a healthier brain and immune system and mood stabilisation, a fat-based metabolism wins every time. Keeping your blood sugar, insulin and leptin levels low are among the most reliable markers of longevity there are.

> 'If there is a known single marker for long life, as found in the centenarian and animal studies, it is low insulin levels.'
>
> *Dr Ron Rosedale,* Specialist in nutritional and metabolic medicine

GUT HEALTH

One of the great casualties of the modern way of eating has been the health of our gut. Every single physiological and biochemical process in your body and brain is dependent upon the nutrients and the quality of the nutrients that you supply them with. Even so, you can be eating the best-quality nutrient-dense diet there is but if you have poor digestion and/or assimilation all those wonderful nutrients will do you little good. You can't effectively supply your body with all that good nutrition unless you are able to digest and absorb it properly. Right? For this we need a healthy gut. Unfortunately, many people today suffer from all kinds of digestive issues, and eating a poor diet to begin with only makes things worse.

When discussing your gut, it's important to know that it is comprised of:

- your stomach (where most of the initial digestion of dietary proteins occurs) and whether or not it is producing enough hydrochloric acid and something called intrinsic factor that you need to properly absorb vitamin B12;
- your small intestine (where more refined enzymatic digestion and nutrient assimilation occurs);
- your gallbladder (which helps you digest dietary fats and fat-soluble nutrients);
- your large intestine (where water is reabsorbed and where critical bacterial processing of digestive waste occurs);
- your microbiome (the kinds of bacteria inhabiting it);
- your brain.

Huh? What does your brain have to do with any of this?

Digestion is actually a 'north to south' process in your body and always starts with your brain and nervous system and whether or not you happen to be in an appropriate parasympathetic (calm and relaxed) state where digestion can actually occur.

The brain is also responsible for the appropriate hormonal signalling and communication with your gut that can help it know what it needs to do at the right time. Taking the time to relax and really focus on the taste and aroma of your food is an important first step when it comes to actually digesting it.

I introduced the paleo way of eating to my household 10 months ago because I am intolerant to gluten and fructose and my partner has always suffered from gut problems. We both feel so much better since adopting this lifestyle. We also spend more time together as a family – growing, cooking and enjoying yummy food. Some people have responded negatively to our switch to paleo, but we know that we are teaching healthy eating habits to our kids and that they will one day inspire others to just eat real food!

Timenah, 27 years

HOW DO WE CREATE GOOD GUT HEALTH?

In short: by making sure you give your body the kinds of food it was designed to eat. Also, it is important to make sure that you are supporting the health of the microorganisms in your gut that help it – and the rest of your body and immune system – stay healthy. Making your own homemade cultured and fermented foods (like sauerkraut, coconut kefir and yoghurt) can be wonderful additions to your diet that add new beneficial, healthy bacteria to your gut each and every day. They're easy, delicious and, if you make your own, extremely affordable. If you already have digestive symptoms, you may need to find a knowledgeable medical practitioner to do a thorough evaluation of your symptoms so that you have a better idea of where to start and what you need to do and, more specifically, prioritise. Remember: until your gut is working at its best you can never make the most of even the healthiest diet.

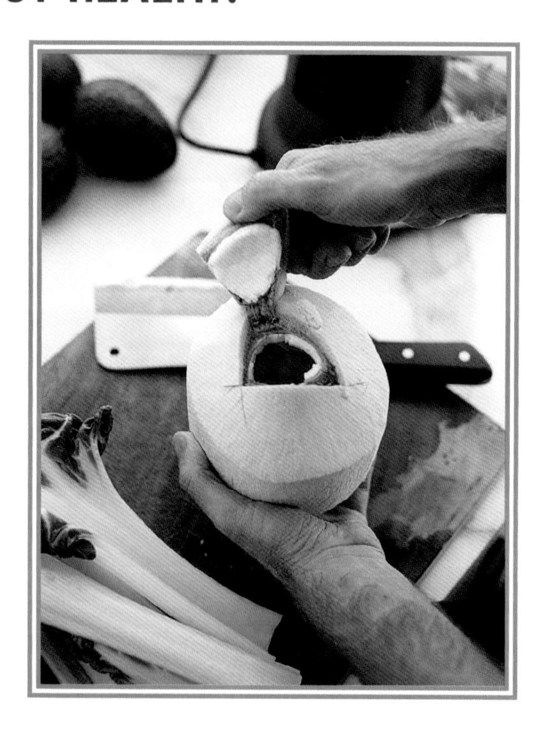

GRAINS AND YOUR GUT

Keeping your gut flora happy can be one of the most important keys to your health and wellbeing. In fact, these critters that you harbour in your gut outnumber us manyfold. This might be hard to believe, but it turns out that as much as 99 per cent of all the cells in your body aren't even human! We all have more 'alien' DNA from non-human microorganisms occupying our bodies than we do human DNA and cells. And those microorganisms can make or break your health. Be nice to them.

The human genome contains roughly 23,000 genes but the microorganisms in your gut add another mind-blowing five to ten million genes beyond that. This seemingly silent majority within you – mostly in your lower intestine – is responsible for being your immune system's first line of defence. They help detoxify and synthesise a number of important nutrients in your body, including some fat-soluble vitamins (even influencing vitamin D receptor expression) and fatty acids, plus methylated folate – the body's most usable and important form of folic acid. Some of these microorganisms can strongly influence your mood and brain function, and whether you are able to lose weight or not. Some less-friendly varieties of bacteria can lead you to having a chronically leaky gut by secreting certain toxic compounds called lipopolysaccharides (LPS).

Ideally, at least 85 per cent of your gut should be made up of the good guys (healthy probiotic flora) and no more than 15 per cent bad guys (pathogens).

A particular gut bacteria species known as Prevotella seem to be associated with whole grain consumption, according to anthropologist, microbiome specialist, researcher and head of the Human Food Project Dr Jeffery Leach. It's interesting to point out that elevated levels of Prevotella have been noted among HIV-infected individuals who exhibit chronic gut inflammation. In one study, the researchers suggested that Prevotella may thrive under conditions of inflammation.[22] In yet another study, researchers found that Prevotella strongly correlated with new-onset, untreated rheumatoid arthritis.[23]

The main lectin in wheat (wheat germ agglutinin or WGA) has catastrophic effects upon the gastrointestinal tract.[24] WGA can also – with no associated immune reactivity – cross the human blood–brain barrier, attach itself to myelin and block nerve growth factor, effectively damaging the brain without any immune modulated reactivity. This is a wake-up call for anyone consuming wheat – regardless of genetic susceptibility or immunologic vulnerability to grains.[25] The richest source of WGA, by the way, lies in the supposedly healthy whole grains and sprouted grain breads.

Immune-reactivity to wheat and gluten (a particular protein contained in certain grains) has been growing exponentially in recent years. Renowned coeliac researcher Dr Alessio Fasano has stated that: 'Although we've been eating wheat for thousands of years, we are not engineered to digest gluten … We don't have the enzymes to dismantle it completely, leaving undigested peptides that can be harmful. The immune system may perceive them as an enemy and mount an immune response.'[26]

Even gluten-free grains can be a source of immune reactivity as they are rich in adversely immune-provoking lectins and proteins also foreign to the human genome. Many gluten-free grains have a known cross-reactive effect with gluten sensitivity, unknowingly yielding a gluten-like immune reaction in some. The storage and processing of all forms of grain additionally present frequent dangers of gluten cross-contamination. Additionally, all grains, despite their questionably utilisable protein content, are a predominantly starch-based food high in lectins, potentially immune-reactive proteomes, mineral-depleting phytates and other antinutrients linked to metabolic dysregulation, obesity, diabetes, heart disease, cancers, autoimmunity and gastrointestinal disorders.

A MODERN DAY EPIDEMIC

Both coeliac disease and gluten immune reactivity are becoming epidemic problems in the general populace. It is one of the most common lifelong disorders in the Western world and can potentially trigger over 100 autoimmune diseases and gluten immune reactivity can affect any area of the body. The latest numbers indicate that as many as one in every five people (yes, that's right) have some form of gluten sensitivity.

A very large study published in the Journal of the American Medical Association in 2009 found that people with diagnosed, undiagnosed and latent coeliac disease or gluten sensitivity had a higher risk of death, mostly from heart disease and cancer.[27] In effect, all forms of gluten immune reactivity have comparable adverse effects when it comes to impacts upon health and longevity. Coeliac disease is only the tip of the proverbial iceberg when it comes to the impact of gluten on your body.

In what was likely the largest epidemiological study related to coeliac disease to date, more than 13,000 subjects were screened for the associated antibodies. Those who tested positive underwent further blood tests and, when possible, a small-bowel biopsy to confirm the presence of coeliac disease. The results, published in 2003, were stunning: one in every 133 people had coeliac disease. And among those related to coeliac patients, the rates were as high as one in 22. These statistics relate solely to enteropathic (gut-based) coeliac disease, now recognised to be a mere fraction of those suffering the impact of non-enteropathic (outside the gut) coeliac-related tissue damage. And coeliac disease as a whole comprises only about 12 per cent of what actually constitutes a broader issue of gluten immune reactivity.[28] We are looking at a true epidemic, despite the fact that only 1–3 per cent of gluten immune reactivity sufferers are ever diagnosed. Do not mistake this statistic, however, for the oft-stated notion that only 1–3 per cent of the population is affected. Those numbers are far higher.

Even in lieu of having an immune reactivity to gluten, all people eating it generate the enzyme zonulin in response, which adversely impacts on gut permeability and blood–brain barrier permeability and poses a degree of risk to developing immune reactivity, as well as potential cognitive, mood and neurological issues.[29]

All this clearly and obviously establishes that eliminating grains from your diet will not pose any health-related risks. In fact, it is clear that grains are more likely to cause problems than support your best possible health.[30] Are we really putting ourselves at risk by rejecting grains? Or are we merely endangering the enormous profits of big agribusiness and the food industry (and those they educate) by prioritising our own health over their bottom line?

AVOIDING LEGUMES

Like grains, legumes, are a very new food to our species. In the wild, they are toxic and were not consumed in any meaningful way by our Palaeolithic ancestors. Legumes, such as soy, were introduced into the human diet (and even then only as a fermented condiment) about 2000 years ago in China.[31] Early agriculturalists worked hard to breed the toxic compounds out of certain varieties of legumes so they could be consumed. However, toxic compounds still remain in modern day cultivated varieties and may cause many health problems in those who frequently consume them.[32,24]

Nutritionally, legumes are inferior in their protein, vitamin and mineral content to animal source foods and they may contain as much as 60 per cent starch – making them a primarily high carb rather than a high protein food. Beans do have more protein than, say, broccoli but this is a far cry from making them a true (or complete) protein food. Australian Government guidelines lump legumes in with meat, poultry, fish and eggs as a viable source of protein. Yet legumes contain a good 66 per cent less protein than chicken or turkey, and 61 per cent less protein than beef, pork or seafood.[33,34] Furthermore, the proteins in legumes are nowhere near as digestible or utilisable as protein from animal source foods and they are extremely poor in levels of the important amino acids methionine and cysteine, which are critical for our health and normal internal protein synthesis.[35,36,24]

The presence of minerals such as zinc, calcium, magnesium and iron in legumes in no way implies that these minerals are available by eating them. The very high phytates and other antinutrient content in legumes make the minerals not particularly available (as they bind to the phytates, saponins, tannins and fibre). Eat enough legumes and they can deplete your body's mineral stores.[37,38,39,40]

All legumes, such as beans, peas, lentils, peanuts and soybeans, contain substances that include concentrated levels of lectins (toxic, inflammatory, immune and hormone-dysregulating compounds that can also damage your gut) and can seriously compromise your health.[41,42,43,44,45,46,32,47,48,49] Plants – not having teeth, claws or legs with which to thwart or escape potential predators – developed lectins as a potent defence against animals (including us) eating them.[50] All varieties of beans (black beans, kidney beans, pinto beans, green beans, navy beans etc.) within the Phaseolus vulgaris species contain an extremely toxic lectin called phytohaemagglutinin (PHA), which has damaging cumulative effects.[51,52,53] Basically, the more PHA you eat the less healthy you become. Cooking may lessen the concentrations of PHA but it doesn't eliminate them completely. The highest PHA levels of all are found in soy.

Then there are phytates ... lots and lots of them. Phytates (also called phytic acid) bind minerals in a way that makes them difficult to absorb and, if you eat enough legumes, can even promote mineral deficiencies. Despite what seems like a decent amount of iron and zinc in beans, the minerals may only be 25 per cent available, at best.[54,55,56,57,58] And it takes the presence and sufficient production of hydrochloric acid to ionise and properly absorb those minerals.

Protease inhibitors in legumes can make it extremely difficult to digest and utilise protein over time and may stress your pancreas.[59,60,31,61] Goitrogens (substances that can impair thyroid function) are found in high concentrations in legumes, particularly soy. Isoflavones, a form of phytoestrogen, can actually cause goitres, together with depressed thyroid function in people who consume a significant amount of soy. A meta-analysis of 47 studies showed that women consuming soy daily suffered significant drops (20 per cent) in two female hormones luteinizing hormone (LH) and follicle stimulating hormone (FSH). In another study looking at the influence of soy, six weeks of consumption by women led to depressed LH plus a cessation of ovulation.[62] The implications of this become even more concerning when related to maternal diets during pregnancy and the iodine and thyroid impairing effects that may lead to adverse issues in babies.[63]

Other antinutrients in legumes, such as saponins, can damage your gut and your blood cells and interfere with protein digestion.[64,65,66,67,68,69]

Of all legumes, soybeans contain more mineral depleting phytates than any other. Also many soybeans grown today are genetically modified (GMO) and commercial soybean oil is nearly always partially hydrogenated, making it a source of trans fats. Tragically, hydrogenated soybean oil is used widely in processed foods, bottled salad dressings and most restaurants and fast food places. This oil should be avoided by everyone who cares about their health. Entire books have been devoted to meticulously outlining the innumerable reasons why soy should be avoided by pretty much everyone.[70]

A particular lectin in peanuts (which, by the way, are a legume not a nut) and peanut oil, called peanut oil lectin or PNA, is actually a very potent initiator of atherosclerosis (arterial disease).[71,72,73,74]

Cyanogenic glycosides, found in lima beans, produce hydrogen cyanide when you eat them, which can be lethal if poorly cooked or can become thyroid impairing when cooked.[75] Red kidney beans are especially dangerous when not thoroughly cooked and their import is even banned in some places due to health-related concerns.[76,77,78,79] Broad beans (fava beans) contain favism glycosides, which are a highly toxic and potentially lethal compound that creates acute haemolytic anaemia.

It is true that some antinutrients in certain legumes can be neutralised or partially neutralised by careful soaking and cooking or by the process of fermenting. Even so, that doesn't necessarily take care of all the potential issues associated with eating them and it certainly doesn't transform them into a health food.[52] The fact remains, many people experience some degree of discomfort from the consumption of even well-cooked legumes; this should be the first hint that we as humans were simply not designed to digest or eat them.

All nutrients in legumes may be found elsewhere in a quality legume-free diet, and with fewer potential consequences. There is nothing in legumes that is essential to anyone, but there is quite a bit in them that can cause some real problems.

All nutrients in legumes may be found elsewhere in a quality legume-free diet, and with fewer potential consequences.

THE ROLE OF ANIMAL FATS

As I've already discussed, animal fats have always played a critical role in our diet and an absolutely pivotal role in our brain's development.

So what kind of fat does the human brain like? A peek at what fats make up our brains should give us a few clues. It turns out that roughly half of the human brain is made up of saturated fat; about 11 per cent is arachidonic acid, found exclusively in animal source foods; 25 per cent of the fatty acids in your brain are docosahexaenoic acid (DHA), also found in animal source foods and poorly synthesised (if at all) from any plant sources of omega-3s we might have consumed. Furthermore, one-quarter of all the cholesterol in our bodies lies within our brains, where it is utterly essential for cognitive functioning. One of the very worst things you can do to your brain is avoid or try to excessively lower cholesterol. Cholesterol actually protects your nerve cells and speeds the brain's operation in all areas, including thought process, recall and speech. It is also the building block for synapses (the areas between cells that transmit messages).

Older people with low total cholesterol (under 200 mg/dL) are much more likely to perform poorly on tests of mental function than those with high cholesterol (over 240 mg/dL).[80] Also, low levels of cholesterol in the brain are commonly associated with endocrine issues, depression, anxiety, mood problems/mood swings, attention disorders (ADD/ADHD, etc.), cognitive dysfunction, poor memory, Alzheimer's and other dementias and neurological instability, which can include greater susceptibility to seizures (for those already prone) and greater susceptibility to migraines.

We only recently – within the last 200 years or so – began consuming processed vegetable oils (other than olive oil and coconut oil). Most of these oils are extremely high in omega-6s which, although essential, when eaten in excess lead to increased inflammation and impaired use of critical omega-3s, such as EPA and DHA (both animal source omega-3s we need for healthy brain and immune function).

A diet rich in dietary fat from a variety of natural sources is automatically rich in critical fat-soluble nutrients – vitamins A (retinol), D3, E, K2 – which are nutritional superstars. These active fat-soluble nutrients, mostly if not exclusively found in animal source foods, initiate and modify your gene expression and have a uniquely powerful role in promoting health and avoiding disease. These vitamins are directly able to enter the nuclei in your cells, bind to nuclear receptors and modify the way your genes are transcribed. So can this happen if you eat a low-fat diet? The fact is that no one can absorb dietary fat-soluble nutrients without the sufficient and regular presence of dietary fat. They all have to work together. Fat in your body rules – and the type and quality of fat counts.

WHY ORGANIC?

From 2.6 million years ago to before World War I everything we ate came from fresh, unprocessed, organic, wild-caught and pasture-fed sources, all untainted by pesticides, herbicides, GMOs, synthetic fertilisers, radiation, pasteurisation, hormones, antibiotics and who knows what else. We evolved eating a 100 per cent natural and uncontaminated diet. This is the way of eating we were designed for.

In pre-agricultural times our planet's rich topsoil maintained and rejuvenated itself through the action and cycles of grazing animals (and their predators, which influenced their continuous movement) upon the land. These grazing animals fertilised the land and aerated it with their hooves, leaving stronger root systems and healthy watersheds in their wake. Grazing animals, their natural predators and our planet's grasslands co-evolved, after all. Once we came along and removed grazing animals from the grasslands and put them in confined areas, the progressive deterioration towards erosion and desertification began, ultimately leading to drought, vast environmental degradation and human famine. The mere act of putting plough to soil initiated the inevitable process of soil degradation, leading to the loss of our repository of critical minerals. It has also inexorably led us to the depleted, vulnerable and weakened state in which we find ourselves today.

Right now the only way to avoid exposure to adulterated food is to buy and eat organically. Some people see the term organic as some sort of elitist moniker, when, in fact, it is a way of eating that used to be the only kind of food available to us. Access to clean, nutrient-dense, sustainably/humanely raised and unadulterated food should not be considered an elite privilege – it should be a fundamental human right.

We have faced an industrialised food supply now for roughly 200 years – less than 13 generations of unprecedented forays into entirely novel ways of eating and treating our food, soil, air, water, environment and food animals. This has clearly not been without dire consequence for us. Exposure to pesticides and herbicides (and toxic compounds like glyphosate found in the widely used garden products) doesn't kill you quickly – it's more cruel and subtle (and less traceable) and happens over time. Instead, you die slowly from cancer, Parkinson's disease or complications related to autoimmunity.

ARE ORGANIC FOODS REALLY HEALTHIER?

In 2009, the American Association for the Advancement of Science featured a presentation on soil health and its impact on food quality. Their conclusion? Healthy soil leads to higher levels of nutrients in crops.[81,82] On average, organic foods contain a 25 per cent higher concentration of 11 nutrients than their conventional counterparts.[83]

Another study – this one commissioned by the Organic Retailers and Growers Association of Australia (ORGAA) – found that conventionally grown fruit and vegetables purchased in supermarkets and other commercial retail outlets had ten times less mineral content than fruit and vegetables grown organically. The Australian Government Analytical Laboratory also analysed a similar range of vegetables grown conventionally and purchased from a supermarket.[84] Organically grown vegetables and fruit ultimately have significantly more antioxidants, polyphenols, and enzymes than conventional produce.[85,86,87,88,89]

I have been gluten-free for a number of years, but until recently I still ate a lot of processed foods. I did a cooking workshop last year and have since changed the way I eat. I now only buy organic meat, eggs, fruit and vegetables whenever possible. I cook with coconut oil and focus on eating natural wholefoods. Since changing my diet I have lost weight and have clearer skin. I also have much more energy and look and feel healthier.

Emma, 35 years

According to a 2004 report in *The Journal of the American College of Nutrition*, levels of calcium, riboflavin, vitamin C, iron, potassium and protein in vegetables and fruit have significantly declined since 1950.[90] Practices such as selectively breeding for product size and sweetness, picking produce prematurely (then later ripening it through gassing with ethylene to improve shelf life, thus limiting the beneficial, cancer-fighting nutrient-enhancing benefits associated with sun-ripening) and the use of synthetic fertilisers may deplete the vitamin C content of your produce.[91,92,93,94,95,96,97]

The cost of not buying organic goes well beyond just losing out on nutrient density

A behavioural study conducted found greater risk of ADHD in children with higher levels of organophosphate (OP) pesticides.[98] Another study published in Environmental Health Perspectives showed that consuming organic products may significantly lower children's exposure to potentially damaging pesticides.[99] A previous study by members of the study team had shown that children eating primarily organic diets had significantly lower OP pesticide exposure than did children consuming primarily conventional diets. In fact, an earlier study found no measurable pesticide metabolites in the urine of a child whose family bought exclusively organic produce.[100]

Industry tries (and fails) to pull a fast one

A large and supposed meta-analyses study performed by scientists at Stanford University (heavily funded by Cargill – a major proponent of GMOs) looked at 240 reports comparing organically and conventionally grown food (including 17 human studies). There was considerable and controversial evidence that the researchers in this study (some of whom had been hired decades ago to disprove the harmfulness of tobacco) were clearly biased in favour of the big agribusiness interests that funded them and pressured the researchers to undermine any findings in favour of organic foods. Even so, these results clearly showed that organic foods are, in fact, safer and healthier than conventional foods – assuming of course you are of the rational conviction that ingesting fewer toxins is healthier and safer for you. One tremendous and inarguable benefit of organically grown foods is consuming and ultimately bio-accumulating fewer toxins in your body. Even the food industry lapdogs couldn't prove otherwise.

Can we really afford this?

Although we are all exposed to chemicals, it seems a rational supposition that the name of the game is minimising exposure wherever possible. Choosing to eat organically is one conscious choice we can all make to better safeguard our health and give ourselves a fighting chance to minimise our own and our children's toxic burden. Organic foods and labelling are among our only reasonably reliable safeguards against unwitting exposure to the health-compromising contaminants lurking in our food supply.

Organic vegetables and fruit show significantly higher levels of antioxidants than their conventionally grown counterparts, according to findings published by researchers led by food scientist Alyson Mitchell at the University of California at Davis. Antioxidant levels in sustainably grown corn were 58.5 per cent higher than conventionally grown corn and sustainably and organically grown strawberries had about 19 per cent more antioxidants than their conventional counterparts. The study also showed sustainably grown and organic produce had more ascorbic acid, which the body converts to vitamin C.[87] Findings from a Danish double-blind randomised, crossover study showed organic vegetables have a higher concentration of natural antioxidants called flavonoids.[101]

Organic vegetables and fruit show significantly higher levels of antioxidants than their conventionally grown counterparts.

At the 2005 International Congress Organic Farming, Food Quality and Human Health, Professor Carlo Leifert of Newcastle University reported findings that organically produced food had higher levels of specific antioxidants and lower mycotoxin levels than conventional samples, and that grass-based cattle diets reduce the risk of E. coli contamination while grain-based conventional diets increase the risk.[102] Indeed, the benefits of 100 per cent organic grass-fed meat go well beyond its superior nutrient profile to that of feedlot meat. As a way of avoiding exposure to acid-resistant E. coli, choosing that 100 per cent grass-fed burger or steak could just save your life.

A NOTE ON GMOs

In the last few decades we have been dealing with the advent of genetically modified organisms (GMOs) – unnaturally splicing the genes of animals, insects and plants together – as though nothing could be more reasonable.

GMOs are very much alive and well in Australia, and it will take concerted enlightened consumer purchasing practices, activism, public demand and awareness to bring this dark, potentially health devastating technology into the badly needed light of day. And although GMOs are not technically an official part of the food supply in New Zealand, big agribusiness is already planting 'test plots' of these dangerous crops that threaten to inadvertently infiltrate the healthy food supply through wind pollination. Cross-pollination/contamination such as this has occurred numerous times already and without apology.

The average adult today in Western society may actually eat more than the equivalent of their own body weight in GMO foods each and every year, yet there are zero long-term studies to date verifying their safety. If you were going to eat your weight in something every year, wouldn't you want to be certain it was at least reasonably safe for you and your children, if not actually good for you?

In Australia, companies are required to state on the product label whether there are any GMOs included. In following the paleo way, however, we are avoiding many of the kinds of processed foods that may contain GMOs, which can only be a good thing.

Famous geneticist Dr David Suzuki has stated: 'Any politician or scientist who tells you that these GMO products are safe is either very stupid or lying.' Yep – I'd say that about sums things up.

OCCUPY OUR FOOD

This place we have found ourselves in with respect to global environmental devastation, the collapse of human health, the contamination of our air, water and food supply, the human-generated sixth global mass extinction of species (of which we may well be among), widespread war and famine and the rapid erosion and loss of human civil liberties is attributable to a perfect storm of unbridled power-hungry greed and mainstream human complacency.

Edmund Burke, the Irish political philosopher, once eloquently pointed out that all that is needed in order for evil to triumph is for good men and women to do nothing. It is up to us – yes, you and me, and only you and me – to continue to choose to do nothing or wake in a state of renewed and enlightened awareness and take uncompromising charge of our own food supply, our own health and our own and our children's futures through our choices and unyielding conscious demands and render those seeking to control us for their own selfish and nefarious purposes irrelevant.

It's *all* up to us.

How

YOUR COMPLETE GUIDE *to* GOING PALEO

I am so excited, and extremely humbled, to have you reading this book, as it means the paleo message is getting out there. You too can become as passionate as I am about nourishing the body and mind with healthy and delicious food. I know, first hand, that any lifestyle changes can be really daunting to undertake. So I commend you for taking your first steps on this journey with me. While going paleo might involve a bit of hard work and quite a few changes – from overhauling your kitchen to making different choices when dining out – I guarantee you it will be worth it in the long term.

These changes are the incredible first steps to realising the best version of yourself. Most people who transition to a paleo way of living feel better than they have ever felt before. They lose body fat, gain lean muscle, have a clearer mind and greater mental focus, not to mention clear, glowing skin, sparkling eyes and endless amounts of energy. Going paleo may also help with certain medical conditions like digestion problems, mood and sleep disorders, inflammatory diseases such as arthritis, and some autoimmune diseases.

When faced with challenges in life, I always ask myself the question, 'How will I feel if I don't make these changes?' and then, 'How will I feel if I do make these changes?'. The answer 100 per cent of the time leaves me feeling empowered to dig deep and do whatever it takes to make those initial positive steps in the right direction. It is these positive steps that are the building blocks to success in what you set your mind and body to achieve. So let's get stuck into how we can make this paleo transition period as fun and beneficial as possible.

LISTEN TO YOUR BODY

Your body will change in many ways when you adopt a paleo lifestyle. Listen to your body, allow these changes to happen and embrace them. Physical changes include less body fat, more lean muscle mass and clearer skin, while physiological changes include improved mood, better sleep and appetite control. I want you to observe these changes and to nourish yourself as they happen.

First, I cannot stress enough how vital it is to be in the right headspace when starting on this journey. Any physical transformation in our bodies, both internal and external, must be supported and cultivated through a strong, positive mindset. It is with this mindset that you create the willpower to stick to your guns, to commit to the changes and ultimately to be the person you want to be. So my biggest piece of advice is to create an internal monologue that is loving and caring. Too often we allow negative self beliefs to sneak into our consciousness. These thoughts can derail our best intentions. Remember: you are number one on this phenomenal journey and through your nutritional choices you are creating an amazing future for yourself and those around you. It is important to think positively, be proud, stand tall and love yourself enough to make this investment in your own wellbeing. It will pay off in the short and long term, and will be reflected in all aspects of your life, creating a ripple effect that will rub off on those around you.

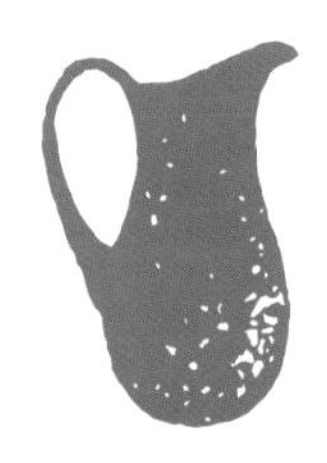

HUNGRY? *Try drinking some water first.*

Dehydration is often mistaken for hunger, so see how you feel after a big glass of water. If you're still hungry, opt for one of the healthy snack options on pages 192–215.

As with any important commitment or event, organisation and preparation are paramount in achieving success. From a practical point of view, the first thing you'll need to do is to overhaul your pantry, fridge and freezer. A lot of everyday ingredients, such as bread, sugar, flour and cow's milk, will have to go – but I've got heaps of helpful advice on alternatives so that you have lots of options at mealtimes. Make a full assessment of your pantry, fridge and freezer to work out what items you need to throw out. Then it's time to make a big list of all the nourishing and healthy ingredients you are going to replace them with (see Setting Up Your Paleo Kitchen, page 62) and make a trip to the health food store and supermarket to stock up. Once your kitchen is well stocked with the right ingredients (and you have removed the temptation of all the wrong ingredients), it will be much easier to eat nutritiously – and you will be well on your way to real health and happiness.

You might also like to start a health journal, detailing the food you eat each day, the exercise you do and how you are feeling. This will make you more aware of the food you are eating and the effect it is having on you. Checking in with your body on a regular basis is a motivating force, as you will clearly see the positive changes that a paleo way of eating brings about. It will also help you to remember how you felt after eating particular foods. If you are following my Kickstart Plan (page 74), it might be a good idea to write up your shopping list and do a big shop on the weekend so that you are all prepped for the week ahead, making it easier to stay on track. And if you've got time on the weekend or in the evenings, why not make some of your snacks or basics (such as Nic's Paleo Bread on page 200 or Spiced Activated Nuts and Seeds on page 198) to give yourself a bit of a head start? If you are time poor, don't worry too much – most of the recipes in this book are really easy to whip up on weeknights, especially if you've already got the ingredients in your kitchen.

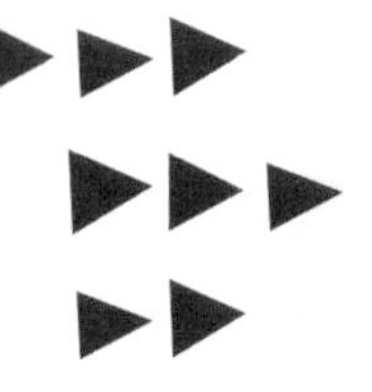

STAYING ACTIVE

Exercise plays a large part in you feeling and looking your best. Ideally you want to be moving in some way every day. This movement should be safe and functional. So whether you are walking the dog, working out in a gym or surfing, do something that keeps your heart healthy, your body active and that, most importantly, you enjoy.

While this book focuses on the eating side of the paleo lifestyle, any paleo eating plan should be partnered with an effective functional movement program to achieve optimum results. A true lifestyle transformation is 80 per cent what you eat and 20 per cent how you move your body. Even making simple changes to your daily routine – like walking or riding part of the way to work instead of driving, or always taking the stairs instead of the lift – can help. There are also heaps of paleo or 'primal movement' exercise programs and trainers out there, so if you're interested, have a look online and find a local group or program to take part in. You will feel so much better once you get outdoors and move your body in a way that is safe and energising.

Surrounding yourself with supportive people can be a huge help on your paleo journey. Having loved ones around you to keep you on track and motivate you can be the difference between succeeding or falling off the wagon. Try to be open to support and allow positive energy into your life. Having said that, you may find that some people around you become detractors and react negatively to your new paleo lifestyle. Too often a person's inability to change, grow and learn means they spend their time and energy bringing others around them down – we call them 'energy vampires'. No one needs negativity around them, so try not to allow it into your life. Control your destiny and create the space and freedom to make what you want happen.

Be out and proud about your transition to paleo

Being out and proud about your paleo lifestyle will encourage those around you to support you. They will take into account your dietary requirements when eating together, whether that's at home or when you are out and about. Support from family and friends can be a massive help when choosing a paleo lifestyle (and you may even get them on board when they see how good you are looking and feeling).

This space and freedom can come not only from the interpersonal relationships in your life but also, in practical terms, from your pantry, fridge and freezer. These three places will either make or break your transition to paleo; and if you can successfully adapt what's in them to suit your new lifestyle, then you are one step closer to achieving unbelievable success. As our relationships sometimes need a clean out so that we remain positive, flourishing people, our kitchens need the same type of clean out, so that every time we make a nutrition-based choice, we are good to go with the right stuff.

GETTING YOUR DAILY ZZZs

Sleep is a vital player in the health and wellness realm. Lack of sleep can affect your food choices, exercise regime and mood. Make sure you get adequate amounts so that your body and soul can rest and recover and function optimally. Many people find that transitioning to the paleo way improves their sleep – a fantastic benefit.

Finally, remember that it's important to consult your doctor or health professional before making any big changes to your diet. They will be familiar with your current health and your medical history. Have a chat with them to double-check that they don't foresee any problems. If you already have known allergies to specific foods, you have a higher chance of having allergies to other foods, so be extra careful when introducing new things into your diet. It may be best to do so in consultation with your health professional. It's also important to note that consuming fermented vegetables as part of your daily diet can be problematic if you have certain medical conditions or are taking particular medications, so again it's always best to consult your health professional before adding them to your diet.

Once you've got the all-clear, it's time to overhaul that kitchen. In the following pages I am going to run through what you need to eliminate, add, swap and use as you eat your way to better health, every day.

Sticking with it

The paleo way is way easier to stick to than other eating programs out there. Why? Because it nourishes your body in all the right ways, making you feel fuller for longer. You will stop eating when you are no longer hungry and will crave the right types of food because you have calibrated your body to make the right choices. When it seems too hard, or you have no option, don't give up. Instead indulge in a paleo treat from time to time if that helps. The way you look and feel will be motivation enough to help you stick to your new paleo lifestyle. Remind yourself why you are doing it and how good you look and feel.

IN AN 'ACTIVATED' NUTSHELL, THE PALEO WAY:

Promotes

- the minimisation of sugary and starchy foods;
- the moderation of protein intake;
- the liberal consumption of fibrous vegetables and greens (raw, lightly cooked and/or fermented/cultured), nuts, seeds and eggs (if tolerated);
- as much dietary natural fat as is needed to satisfy the appetite and support a healthy brain and nervous system;
- an occasional very small amount of seasonal fruit (if desired).

Avoids

- grains, legumes, conventional dairy products, conventionally raised meats, non-organic produce, genetically modified organisms (GMOs) and processed foods.

Embraces

- 100 per cent organic, humanely raised, pasture-fed and finished meats and organs (sustainable as a food supply and healthiest for the human body and the planet).

Advocates

- nose-to-tail eating (all the parts of the animal);
- wild, line-caught seafood from unpolluted waters;
- free-range poultry and pork with no added hormones or antibiotics;
- wild game;
- organically grown produce, nuts, seeds and healthy sources of natural fats.

THE PALEO WAY IS LITERALLY THE MOST NATURAL DIETARY APPROACH ON EARTH, AND THE ONE LIKELIEST TO SUPPORT OPTIMUM PHYSICAL AND EMOTIONAL HEALTH FOR THE BEST QUALITY OF LIFE.

THE THINGS THAT HAVE TO GO *and what to replace them with*

We have become accustomed to eating certain types of food because of what we grew up on, what is advertised in mainstream media and what health authorities tell us we should be eating. Be prepared to have many of the things you know so far be blown out of the water and replaced with clean versions that will give you vitality for life. I have put together a list of some of the main offenders and have given some simple suggestions on what you can replace them with.

1 WHEAT BREAD ➳ *Paleo bread*

Most bread is made from highly processed wheat flour that contains almost no fibre or nutrients and that can cause your blood sugar levels to rise excessively. Not only does grain bread affect your blood sugar levels and insulin, it also contains gluten, lectins and phytates, which can cause digestive problems and prevent your body from absorbing nutrients. When you eat bread, you are filling up on empty carbs and eating fewer nutrient-dense foods, like vegetables and lean meat. I know that bread is one of the hardest things to give up, so I've included a paleo bread recipe (page 200) made with almond meal. It's delicious, doesn't contain any nasties and is perfect with eggs in the morning.

2 SOFT DRINKS AND JUICE ➳ *Water or kefir*

Soft drinks are full of processed sugar and unnatural chemicals, while packaged juice is basically a sugar trap, with all of the sugar but none of the fibre from the fruit. Both drinks can contribute to insulin resistance, weight gain, mood disorders and depression. They add no nutritional value to your diet and should be avoided. The best thing to replace these drinks with is fresh water – so many people don't drink enough of it! To mix things up occasionally, try making some kefir (see recipe, page 228) or drinking the fresh water of a young coconut as a treat. You can buy young coconuts from health food stores, greengrocers and some supermarkets and Asian grocers.

3 PASTA AND RICE ➳ *Zucchini noodles and cauliflower rice*

Pasta and rice fall under the same banner as bread. Digestively, we are not designed to eat them. They are products of the human agricultural revolution, processed foods that contain combinations of gluten, lectins and phytates. Like bread, I know that pasta and rice can be really challenging for people to give up. That's why I've given you a number of cauliflower and broccoli rice recipes (see recipes, pages 109, 124, 141 and 166). And if you are really craving pasta, why not try zucchini noodles (see recipe, page 154) or sautéed kale with your bolognese (see recipe, page 189)?

4 VEGETABLE AND SEED OILS ➳ *Coconut oil*

Highly processed vegetable and seed oils are often made from GMOs and contain high levels of omega-6 fatty acids, which can have a detrimental impact on your health. The problem is, these oils are in nearly every kind of processed food nowadays. Grain-fed livestock (where a lot of meat produce comes from) is also high in omega-6. A diet high in omega-6 is associated with an increase in inflammatory diseases, such as cardiovascular disease, type 2 diabetes, rheumatoid arthritis, asthma and cancer. Coconut oil is really the only oil you want to be cooking with as it can be heated to high temperatures without the nutrient value decreasing. While it is high in saturated fat, it is a special kind of saturated fat consisting of medium-chain triglycerides, which are absorbed easily into the small intestine and therefore less likely to be stored in fatty tissue. Coconut oil is also high in lauric acid, which is found in breastmilk and is both anti-bacterial and anti-fungal.

5 PRE-PACKAGED/BOTTLED SAUCES ➳ *Homemade sauces*

Avoid processed sauces whenever possible. They are some of the worst offenders when it comes to hidden additives. Many low-fat versions contain heaps of sugar, as well as being full of preservatives, artificial chemicals and salt. Cooking a healthy meal and then slathering it with a pre-packaged sauce is undoing all your good work. This doesn't mean you have to forgo sauces altogether – it's easy to make your own healthy versions at home – see pages 238–252 for some recipes.

CHIPS, CRACKERS AND BISCUITS ➳ *Activated nuts and seeds*

There's no way to put this gently – chips, crackers and biscuits have to go. They are full of bad fats, salt, empty carbs, sugars and artificial colours and flavours, and provide very little nutritional benefit. We don't really have an off switch for these types of foods, which is why we can just eat and eat and eat them. And the more we eat of these snack foods, the fewer healthy, nutrient-rich foods we end up eating. Swap these processed foods for Spiced Activated Nuts and Seeds (see recipe, page 198), a few Hard-boiled Eggs (see recipe, page 197) or any of the other recipes in the Snacks chapter (pages 195–215).

CANE SUGAR ➳ *Green stevia leaf*

Most of us know the reasons why we should be avoiding sugar – excess sugar promotes insulin resistance and metabolic diseases, it's bad for our teeth, our gut and heart health as well as our waistlines. Most of the sugar in your diet should be coming from vegetables and the occasional piece of fruit, but if you do feel the need to substitute sugar with something while you are transitioning, then green stevia leaf is your best bet. The green stevia leaf is sweet without containing any sugar or carbohydrates. Make sure you go easy though, as it reminds your body of its sweet cravings. Look for green stevia leaf powder, which is made from pure stevia leaf, rather than the highly refined white powder that is made from stevia extract. Green stevia leaf powder is available from health food stores.

GRAIN FLOURS ➳ *Coconut flour or almond meal*

Almond meal and coconut flour are awesome substitutes for wheat flour when making bread, biscuits, crumbs and more! They are packed full of vitamins and minerals, and don't have any of the negative side effects associated with traditional wheat flour and wheat-flour products. Coconut flour is much more absorbent than wheat flour though; so you'll need less of it (or more liquid). Almond meal gives a really lovely moist texture to muffins and bread.

9 PEANUT BUTTER ➳ *Pure nut butter*

Most peanut butter is packed with added sugar, salt and vegetable oils, not to mention the fact that peanuts aren't actually a nut, they are a legume. Replacing store-bought peanut butter with pure nut butter (using healthier nuts such as almonds, brazil nuts, macadamias or a mix of a number of different nuts) provides you with protein, healthy mono-unsaturated fats and heaps of vitamins and minerals. To make your own nut butter, see page 67.

10 COW'S MILK ➳ *Nut milk*

We avoid dairy in a paleo lifestyle, as lactose is difficult to digest and it contains fatty acids that can increase blood cholesterol. Nut or seed milks are a great substitute for cow's milk, and they are so easy to make (see recipe, page 226). If you don't have time to make your own, you can buy almond milk at the supermarket or health food store. Just be careful though, as many brands have added sugar, which you want to avoid.

11 CREAM ➤ *Coconut cream*

Cream should be avoided for all the same reasons as milk, but it's easy to replace it with coconut cream, which is packed full of good fats and tastes delicious. Blend coconut cream with flavours such as vanilla or cinnamon to jazz it up.

12 HUMMUS ➤ *Tahini*

Hummus is made from chickpeas, which we avoid while following a paleo lifestyle as, being a legume, they are difficult to digest and prevent us from absorbing other nutrients. Commercial brands of hummus often blend the chickpeas with poor-quality oils, which makes things even worse. Instead of hummus, I love to use tahini, which is made from ground sesame seeds and is rich in calcium, protein, B vitamins and good fats. It is perfect for using in sauces and dressings and can be spread on Paleo Bread (see recipe, page 200) or veggie sticks for a healthy snack.

13 COFFEE ➤ *Herbal tea*

Coffee is a stimulant that you just won't need in your life once you balance your health and wellness. You can still keep the ritual and replace your coffee with a delicious herbal tea (up to two cups a day is fine). Not only does it give you the same comforting sensation, you gain many other amazing health and digestive benefits (to read more about different herbal teas and their benefits, see page 65).

Try replacing your daily coffee with a herbal tea (see recipe, page 222).

14 OAT AND GRAIN-BASED BREAKFAST CEREALS ➤ *Paleo muesli*

Most breakfast cereals on the market feature highly processed grains and a huge amount of added sugar. They also offer very little nutritionally. Instead of starting out on the wrong foot, begin your day with paleo muesli (see recipe, page 101). It's packed full of nuts and seeds to provide energy-boosting good fats, vitamins and minerals. Combine this with some coconut cream or nut milk (see recipe, page 226) and you are good to go!

TESTIMONIALS

I stumbled across paleo by accident in 2011. I was already eating a diet that was low in sugar and full of wholefoods, organic produce and good fats; however, I was still obese and suffered from many health complaints. When I read about the results of people who had done the Whole30 (a 30-day paleo program) I thought I'd give it a go, even though I was sceptical about my ability to achieve these results. After two weeks I was hooked! My arthritis symptoms were gone, as was my psoriasis, hormonal imbalance and mood swings. I also lost 35 kg in six months and have kept it off. *Michelle, 44 years*

I was introduced to the paleo way 15 months ago. It started out as a six-week challenge – my trainer wanted me to 'just see what would happen' in terms of my energy levels and my performance at training. I was feeling great at the six-week mark, but then I had one non-paleo meal – some seafood pasta, salad, bread and cake for my mum's birthday. The car trip home after this meal was one of the worst of my life – I had a headache, blurry vision and nausea. I realised that if some foods have the power to affect my body in this way, I really shouldn't be eating them. Since then, I have adapted a paleo lifestyle to suit my own body and lifestyle. Eating this way has increased my energy levels. I am more focused at training and at uni, I've lost weight, my hair and skin are better than they've ever been and I appreciate food more now. The anti-inflammatory benefits have also been outstanding – I no longer find little niggles in my body from training and recover faster than ever before. *Andia, 22 years*

My partner and I have been living a paleo/primal lifestyle now for nearly three years (though we do still eat a small amount of dairy). We both have gone from pre-diabetic to having completely normal test results. I have also been able to come off my heartburn/reflux medication and we have each lost about 15 kg. We find this the easiest way to live and have no problems sticking to the paleo way of eating. We even spent a month travelling through Italy and had no problems in sticking with the paleo way. Nearly all processed food has gone from our diet and we both look and feel so much better than we did three years ago. *Lynda, 58 years*

I have been a gym owner and yoga teacher for over 30 years, and have seen and tried every diet going – each time I lost weight only to regain it. It was only six months ago I changed to a 100 per cent paleo lifestyle and I researched the hell out of it before starting. Within two weeks all of my aches, pains and other conditions had almost gone. Within six weeks I had lost 8 kg of pure belly fat and had an energy level beyond belief. I am now spreading the word through lectures and workshops and the money is donated to local charities. I feel so alive, strong, focused and well. *Jayne, 55 years*

THE PALEO PLATE

FATS Eat as much good-quality, natural fat as you need to satisfy your appetite and support a healthy brain. Good options include coconut oil, extra-virgin olive oil, avocados, olives, duck fat, tallow and lard.

NUTS, SEEDS AND EGGS Eat a moderate amount of nuts, seeds and eggs (if tolerated).

VEGETABLES Eat as many fibrous, non-starchy vegetables as you like. Green, leafy vegetables are particulary good, and try to incorporate a spoon of fermented veggies into every meal.

WATER Drink at least 2 litres of water every day to stay hydrated.

FRUIT An occasional very small amount of seasonal sweet fruit is purely optional.

PROTEIN Eat a moderate amount of protein in the form of humanely-raised, organic meat and organs, sustainable line-caught seafood and free-range poultry and pork.

WE AVOID

DAIRY

LEGUMES

GRAINS

PROCESSED FOODS AND REFINED SUGAR

NOTE: This diagram is intended purely as a guide. Please consult your health practitioner before making any major changes to your diet.

SETTING UP YOUR PALEO KITCHEN

One of the best ways to succeed in your transition to a paleo way of eating is, with a bit of preparation, making sure that your pantry, fridge and freezer are stocked with loads of healthy ingredients. This way it will be easy to avoid temptation and to make every meal and snack a nourishing and delicious one. So, here is my list of paleo essentials to stock up on. Many of these ingredients are available at supermarkets and greengrocers, though for some items you may need to make a trip to the health food store.

PANTRY

OILS AND VINEGARS

Avocado oil

Avocado oil has been linked to the prevention of coronary heart disease, diabetes and prostate problems. Avocado oil has a rich flavour and is lovely drizzled over chargrilled veggies or used in salad dressings.

•••

Coconut aminos

Coconut aminos is made from the raw sap of the coconut tree, which is naturally aged and blended with sea salt. It is a good alternative to soy sauce as it has a higher amino acid content and no gluten. It's also slightly less salty than tamari. I like using coconut aminos and extra-virgin olive oil for dipping paleo bread into when friends come round (see recipe, page 200). Coconut aminos is available from health food stores.

Coconut oil

The unique combination of fatty acids in coconut oil can have positive effects on our health, such as increasing energy expenditure to help us burn more fat and improving brain function. Add a teaspoon to your daily smoothie to pump up the good fat content and use it as a binding agent in frozen raw desserts. I also love to use it in all kinds of cooking – sautéing, grilling, stir-frying and roasting.

•••

Extra-virgin olive oil

Extra-virgin olive oil is great in salad dressings and drizzled over finished dishes. Make sure you always buy extra-virgin, as it is made from the first cold pressing of the olives and you can be absolutely sure that it hasn't been mixed with other poorer quality oils. Extra-virgin olive oil has been linked to a decrease in cancer, heart disease and oxidative stress. Remember though, extra-virgin olive oil becomes unstable at high temperatures and forms potentially harmful compounds, so do not heat it or cook with it or you will lose all its great health properties.

Raw apple cider vinegar

Apple cider vinegar is rich in potassium and is believed to help clear up skin conditions. Bottles of raw apple cider vinegar should contain a 'mother', which has a cobweb-like appearance and is made of healthy enzymes and bacteria. I love using it in dressings and stocks, and also add it to water as the perfect drink to start my day (see recipe, page 220).

Making fat your friend

Fat is a phenomenal source of sustained energy. When reducing your simple carbohydrate intake, you want to look at increasing your good fats through the inclusion of nuts, seeds and cuts of meat. Avocados are also an excellent source of healthy fats and are very easy to add to salads or make into a dip (see recipe, page 210).

SEEDS

Chia seeds

I love adding chia seeds to smoothies and also use them to make a delicious congee or custard for breakfast (see recipes, pages 104 and 92). They are a fantastic source of fibre and protein, contribute to good digestive health and are full of omega-3 fats, which are vital for healthy brain functioning.

Flaxseeds (linseeds)

These are a great source of gluten-free fibre, keeping us nice and regular. Fibre is important in the prevention of bowel cancer, constipation and slowing the absorption of sugar into our blood stream. Try adding flaxseeds to a breakfast blend of nuts and seeds and enjoy with coconut cream or almond milk.

Psyllium husks

Psyllium husks are great for intestinal health. They contain a spongy fibre that reduces appetite, improves digestion and cleanses the system, making them an excellent choice for healthy living. Adding these to a smoothie and to your baking is great for your gut!

Pumpkin seeds

Pumpkins seeds, or pepitas, are great tossed over salad leaves or roasted pumpkin, or simply eaten as a snack on their own. They are rich in zinc, which is important to your body in many ways, including boosting immunity and helping with sleep, mood, and eye and skin health.

Sunflower seeds

Sunflower seeds can be added to salads or sprinkled over roast veggies and they are also an awesome snack. Did you know that sunflower seeds can keep you calm? Yes! The magnesium in sunflower seeds is reputed to soothe the nerves, thus easing stress and migraines and helping you to relax.

SPICES

Chilli

As well as tasting delicious, chilli contains up to seven times the vitamin C of an orange and has a range of health benefits, including aiding digestion and helping to relieve muscle, joint and nerve pain. I use chilli in just about everything. Try rubbing a beautiful piece of red meat with a chilli before barbecuing or adding finely chopped chilli to a salad dressing to liven it up.

•••

Cinnamon

Cinnamon is often used by people with type 2 diabetes as it is thought to improve blood glucose levels. More generally, it's delicious in sweet and savoury dishes and is great for dealing with cravings for naughty food (it tricks your mind into thinking you have had something sweet). I love sprinkling it on top of an almond milk chai and adding it to smoothies.

The spice cupboard

Spices will be your new best friends when getting creative in the kitchen. We have eliminated a lot of pre-packaged sauces and dressings that are often packed full of nasties, so add flavour to your food with a diverse range of spices. By incorporating these flavours, you will never have a bland meal again.

Coriander

Coriander seeds have a lovely, warm citrus flavour when toasted and crushed. They can be used in curries, stews and soups. They contain good levels of minerals such as calcium, iron and magnesium.

•••

Cumin

Cumin is used in many different cuisines, including Indian and Mexican, and is a good source of iron, manganese and other vitamins and minerals. I love tossing ground cumin through mince when cooking up an easy Mexican-inspired dish for the whole family.

•••

Paprika

Paprika is made by grinding capsicums into a fine powder. This amazing spice adds a vibrant red colour and a rich, pungent flavour to a variety of meals. Just a single tablespoon provides ample amounts of several beneficial nutrients, especially carotenoids, a nutrient family that includes vitamin A. Paprika and chicken are a match made in heaven, try it out (see recipe, page 165).

Sumac

Sumac is one of my favourite spices – it is made from crushed sumac berries and has a lovely citrusy tang as well as incredible antioxidant properties. It is widely available at supermarkets and health food stores and makes a fabulous addition to salad dressings.

Turmeric

Turmeric, a natural anti-inflammatory compound, is available in fresh or ground forms and is commonly used in curries. It is now believed that low-level inflammation may play a major role in a number of chronic conditions, such as heart disease, cancer, metabolic syndrome and Alzheimer's. Anything that can help fight inflammation is important. I love adding chopped fresh turmeric to any hot herbal tea.

TEAS

Chamomile

This tea, with its mild sedative effect, is treasured for its ability to relieve insomnia and stress, ease anxiety and encourage a good night's sleep, free of nightmares. It is also great for the skin.

Fennel

With its mild licorice taste, fennel has long been regarded as a powerful digestive aid. It is also used to relieve hypertension and improve milk supply in breast-feeding mothers. Fennel tea is thought to be anti-inflammatory and is a great breath freshener. It is available from health food stores or you can make your own by crushing a teaspoon of fennel seeds using a mortar and pestle and adding them to boiling water.

Ginger

Fresh ginger tea is said to be good for headaches and sore throats and can relieve nausea and motion sickness. It is also believed to have anti-inflammatory properties and a calming effect on the bowels and digestive system. Not to mention it tastes delicious!

Licorice root

Licorice root tea has a natural sweetness, so drinking a cup of it is a great way to curb sugar cravings. It can act as a soothing agent and expectorant, and is also believed to have anti-inflammatory properties. Licorice root tea should be avoided by pregnant women and people who are taking medication for high blood pressure.

Peppermint

When it comes to soothing stress and anxiety, peppermint is one of your best allies. The menthol that is naturally present in peppermint is a muscle relaxant; and the relaxation of muscles can play an important part in natural stress and anxiety relief, not to mention help you to fall asleep. It can also help to relieve colds, headaches and sinus, and aids digestion. I often drink a cup of peppermint tea before bedtime.

FRIDGE

Activated nuts

Well, this takes me back. Remember 2012 anyone, and my 'Day on a Plate' piece, published in *The Age*? My mention of activated almonds caused quite a stir. I am just glad I got the country talking and tweeting. Raw nuts are an awesome and healthy snack, loaded with protein, healthy fats, fibre and important minerals like zinc, magnesium and calcium; however, they contain phytic acid and enzyme inhibitors that can reduce the body's ability to absorb certain nutrients properly. So, what's the answer? Activate them. See my recipe on page 198 for how to do this.

Coconuts

Young coconuts are usually harvested at around 5–7 months and are white in colour. They can be used in so many ways – the water is a good source of potassium and can be enjoyed straight from the coconut, while the flesh can be added to smoothies or used to make a delicious coconut yoghurt (see recipe, page 122). It sometimes takes a bit of practice to open a young coconut! The best way is to cut a circle in the top using a large knife or cleaver and then prise this circle off. Once you've poured the water out (usually about 250 ml), you can scoop out the jelly-like flesh with a spoon. Young coconuts can be found at Asian grocers, health food stores and some supermarkets.

Eggs

Eggs are packed full of protein, vitamins and minerals. Don't be scared to include them in your diet daily, as they promote good cholesterol over the bad stuff. Free-range eggs come from hens housed in a shed that have access to an outdoors area. The standards that these chickens are kept in can really vary, so I always look for pasture-raised, free-range, organic and where possible biodynamic eggs whenever I can. I love eating eggs at any time of day, but they are particularly great for breakfast (see recipes, pages 90, 95 and 98).

Seasonal eating

By eating seasonally you get to try a diverse range of ingredients you may not normally pick up when food-shopping. In addition to adding variety to your eating, it is also way better for the environment. Less pressure is put on farmers to produce fruits and veggies that aren't naturally grown at certain times of the year, which means demand for out-of-season foods will lessen, and farmers can resort to more sustainable agricultural practices.

Fruit

If you are following my Kickstart Program (see page 74), I recommend limiting sugary fruits for the entire time, but embracing non-starchy fruits such as avocados, tomatoes and cucumbers. (You'll see notes on these in the vegetable section, as although they are technically fruits, they are commonly thought of as veggies.) Berries are perfect for adding to smoothies or as a snack with nuts. They are loaded with fibre and top the charts in antioxidant power, protecting your body against inflammation and free radicals (molecules that can damage cells and organs).

•••

Good-quality fats

Lard (pig fat), tallow (beef fat) and duck fat contain saturated and mono-unsaturated fats that are the preferred fuel source for the body. They are also stable at high temperatures and thus the safest fats to cook with. However, with all animal products, please ensure they are from the healthiest, grass-fed animals you can find (at your butcher or online).

•••

Nut milks

Nut milks offer 30 per cent of the recommended daily amount of calcium, as well as 25 per cent of the recommended amount of vitamin D, which helps to reduce the risk of arthritis and osteoporosis and improves your immune function. Plus, these two nutrients work together to provide us with healthy bones and teeth. To make your own, see my recipe on page 226.

SPREADS

Nut butters

I love nut butters, especially almond and macadamia butter. I often spread them on celery for a snack on the go. Almond butter contains vitamins B and E, as well as magnesium, which contributes to bone health, while macadamia butter is rich in healthy mono-unsaturated fats. You can buy nut butter from some supermarkets and health food stores. Or to make your own, simply pop some nuts in a food processor and whiz until you reach your desired consistency. You can also roast the nuts before processing for added flavour.

•••

Tahini

Tahini is a paste made from ground sesame seeds and has a smooth, creamy texture. It is an excellent source of protein, copper and manganese and a good source of calcium, magnesium and iron. I usually opt for unhulled tahini, which has a stronger flavour than the hulled variety. Tahini is great for adding to dressings and sauces, or perfect for dipping veggies into as a snack or spreading on paleo bread (see recipe, page 200).

Food labels

When reading food labels, first make sure there is nothing artificial in the product, including colours, flavours and preservatives. Next, look at the ingredients. If they're not related to the food you are buying, give the product a wide berth. For example, some processed meats are 70 per cent ham mixed with soy-, wheat- and gluten-based fillers. Ideally, you shouldn't need anything from a packet, but if you do choose to buy pre-packaged foods, choose wisely.

CONDIMENTS & SAUCES

Fish sauce

I love using fish sauce in Asian-style dishes, dressings and sauces for the amazing umami flavour it imparts. Traditional fish sauce is made from fermented fish, salt and water. It's widely available from supermarkets and Asian grocers, just make sure you check the label and choose a brand with no added sugar.

Mayonnaise

Homemade mayo is perfect to have on hand. So many store-bought options are packed full of poor-quality oil, emulsifiers and preservatives that you just do not need. So whip some up (see recipe, page 250) and enjoy as a side to your favourite dishes.

Sugar-free or fermented mustard

Mustard is an excellent way to add flavour to your salad dressings and sauces. I love making my own wholegrain fermented mustard (see recipe, page 238) – it's so easy and delicious, with the added bonus of improving gut health. If you don't have time to make your own, you can buy wholegrain or Dijon mustard from health food stores and supermarkets – just make sure you check the label and choose a sugar-free variety. I love my mustard with a beautifully rare piece of red meat.

Sugar-free tomato ketchup

Commercial tomato ketchup is one of the worst offenders when it comes to high levels of sugar and preservatives. Avoid it. And don't let your kids anywhere near it. Instead, make your own (see recipe, page 226). It tastes way better and is way better for you.

Fermented vegetables

The health of our gut is so important and one way to increase the number and variety of healthy bacteria in our digestive system is to eat some fermented veggies each day. You can buy fermented vegetables from health food stores, but it is also truly easy to make your own – see recipes on pages 110, 116 and 121 for ideas.

Meat, poultry and seafood

Quality protein will keep you feeling fuller for longer. And the healthier the animal the healthier the meat will be for you. Always remember to source amazing quality protein, like grass-fed beef, pasture-fed lamb, organic free-range poultry and sustainable line-caught seafood. This will limit your footprint on the planet, help look after our animals and give you way more nutrients from your protein sources.

Embrace aromatics such as lemongrass and fresh turmeric – they will make your dishes and body sing!

GETTING MORE GREENS IN YOUR DIET

Greens such as kale, spinach, beetroot leaves, watercress and chard are packed full of awesome phytonutrients. There are so many wonderful ways to incorporate them – a breakfast tortilla (see recipe, page 102), kale chips as a snack (see recipe, page 203) or autumn greens as a side at dinner (see recipe, page 118). You can also add them to your smoothies (see recipe, page 230).

VEGETABLES

NOTE: *Some of these items, such as avocados, tomatoes and cucumbers, are actually fruits, but are featured here as most people think of them as vegetables.*

Avocado

Many people are surprised that a food high in fat and calories is considered good for weight loss; however, research has shown that mono-unsaturated fatty acids are more likely to be used as slow-burning energy than stored as body fat. This slow-burning energy and the feeling of satiety that you get from eating an avo are two reasons why they are known for reducing appetite. They are perfect drizzled with olive oil and a sprinkle of sea salt, added to salads or made into a delicious dip (see recipe, page 210) or smoothie (see recipe, page 230).

Beetroot

Beetroot is a good source of fibre, magnesium and potassium. I love including some beets in a big tray of roasted veg; they are also great when grated raw into salads. And make sure you don't throw away the beetroot leaves! These are a rich source of calcium, iron, vitamins A and C, and probably even more nutritious than the beets themselves.

Broccoli and broccolini

Broccoli and broccolini are powerful antioxidants with a concentrated source of vitamin C. Try sautéing them with some toasted almonds for a really simple and nutritious lunch or side dish.

Brussels sprouts

Brussels sprouts are one of the most nutritious vegetables around and, as an added bonus, they have a very low glycaemic index. They are a storehouse of several flavonoid antioxidants that together are believed to offer protection from prostate, colon and endometrial cancers. Cooking these up in some bacon fat tastes absolutely delicious.

Cabbage

An excellent source of vitamins K and C, cabbage is a great veggie to include in two or three meals a week. It is fantastic eaten raw – I like slicing it finely and using it in salads – but is also great lightly stir-fried or steamed.

Capsicum

All capsicums are an excellent source of vitamin C. Ripe capsicums – red, yellow and orange ones – are usually sweeter than less ripe green capsicums, but they are also richer in antioxidants. These are one of my favourite veggies to just chop and eat raw with some nut cheese as a healthy snack.

Cucumber

Cucumbers are a great quick pick-me-up as they are a good source of B vitamins. They also rehydrate the body and replenish daily vitamins. So put down your fizzy drinks and coffee and eat some cucumber slices instead. Try adding some cucumber sticks to the kids' lunchboxes for a hydrating and delicious snack.

Daikon

Otherwise known as Japanese radish, daikon is a good source of fibre, vitamin C, folate, potassium and copper. I love eating it raw with some really fresh sashimi (see recipe, page 144) but it also makes a delicious side when cut into slices and lightly simmered in a fish broth.

Eggplant

Eggplants are a good source of fibre, vitamin B1, copper and a host of other nutrients. They are excellent added to curries and stews, and fantastic on the barbecue with lots of garlic.

Herbs will become your new best friend once you've gone paleo!

Herbs

I could not live without herbs! They add amazing flavour to any dish and also pack a powerful nutritional punch. Many herbs, such as rosemary, are very high in antioxidants; basil and sage are excellent sources of vitamin K; and parsley is a true powerhouse food, providing large amounts of vitamins K, C and A, folate and iron, as well as antioxidants. Go crazy with herbs, I say!

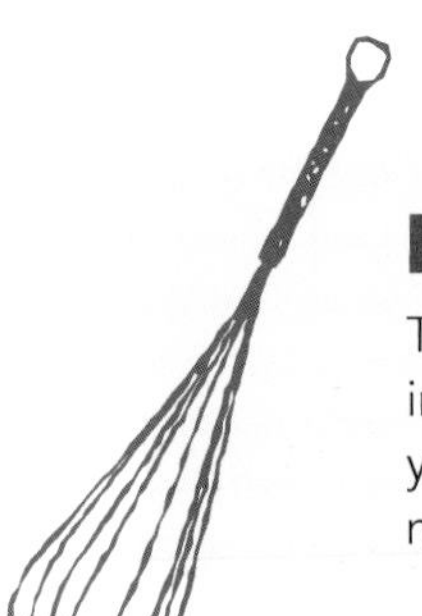

KITCHEN EQUIPMENT

There is no right or wrong when it comes to kitchen equipment. Great investments are a good, safe non-stick frying pan, sharp knives that will help you chop all those veggies with ease and a food processor for making dips, nut butters, dressings, smoothies and more.

Kale and other dark leafy greens

Kale is a nutritional powerhouse. One cup of chopped kale contains 9 per cent of the daily dose of calcium, 206 per cent of vitamin A, 134 per cent of vitamin C and a whopping 684 per cent of vitamin K. It is also a good source of the minerals copper, potassium, iron, manganese and phosphorus. Making kale chips is a great way to use this awesome green veggie and to encourage your kids to eat it (see recipe, page 203). Other dark leafy greens such as cavolo nero, silverbeet and chard are also very nutritionally dense and full of vitamins and minerals.

Mushrooms

I love adding mushrooms to my breakfast fry-up! They have a satisfying texture and rich flavour and are also a good source of copper, selenium and B vitamins. If you're looking for a delicious new way to serve mushrooms for dinner, try stuffing them with pork and garlic (see recipe, page 168). They're out of this world.

Okra

Green okra pods can be found at Asian grocers. They are a good source of fibre, potassium, folate and vitamins C and K. You can slice okra thinly and add it raw to salads. It's also delicious added to soups and stews – just don't freak out if it becomes a bit slimy! Okra is a mucilaginous vegetable so it does produce some slime when cooked but is still absolutely delicious.

Pumpkin

Pumpkin is a bit of an overlooked veggie nutritionally, but it is a great source of fibre, potassium and vitamin A. A tray of roasted veg isn't quite right without some good chunks of pumpkin in there. Leftover roast pumpkin can be used to make a delicious salad – just add avocado, rocket leaves, herbs, toasted nuts and a dressing of your choice (see recipes, pages 238–241).

A few whole, crunchy radishes make a refreshing snack.

Radishes

Crunchy red radishes are one of my favourite veggies to slice thinly and add to a fresh salad. They have a natural spiciness and fabulous crisp texture. They're also a good source of vitamin C, potassium and folate.

Tomatoes

Tomatoes are high in alpha-lipoic acid, which helps the body to convert glucose into energy. They are at their best in summer and I love combining them with pomegranate seeds for a delicious salad (see recipe, page 128).

Watercress

Watercress is an unexpected powerhouse veggie. Recent research has shown it to be the most nutritionally dense leafy green vegetable, with the ability to reduce DNA damage to cells, which is a trigger in the development of cancer. Add it to salads, sprinkle it over your eggs in the morning or even eat it on its own!

Zucchini

Zucchini has a high water content and is really low in calories, so you can happily eat as much as you want. It also provides decent amounts of fibre and protein, and excellent levels of vitamin C, potassium and manganese. While most people cook zucchini in curries, stews and stir-fries, it can be enjoyed raw in a Thai-influenced salad (see recipe, page 127) or fermented with a range of other veggies (see recipe, page 116).

Embracing the old-fashioned roast for dinner

Did you know that the humble roast dinner is an amazing paleo meal that families have been enjoying for generations? It has high-quality protein, good fats and a healthy dose of veg alongside. This is just one of the many traditional meals you probably already know that are actually really paleo friendly, which will make your transition a whole lot easier!

FREEZER

Back-up meals

These are great to have on hand if you are running late from work or your week gets away from you and you do not have time to prep properly. (Preparation is key to making the paleo way work for you.)

Berries

Berries are high in fibre and antioxidants. They are always great to have on hand for recipes and smoothies.

Bone broths/stocks

Not all broths or stocks are created equal. Store-bought stocks and broths are often packed full of added sodium and preservatives. If I don't have homemade bone broth, I simply use water instead. The benefits of bone broths are many and varied – they contain numerous minerals, such as magnesium and phosphorus, that are in a form readily absorbed by your body; they contain glucosamine from the broken-down cartilage and tendons, which helps with joint pain and arthritis; and they can help to heal the lining of your gut, among many other things. It's really easy to make your own bone broths using leftover bones and veggies, and it also minimises waste. See my recipes for bone broths on pages 255–258.

Meat, fish, chicken, liver, marrow, offal

To help you stay on track with your healthy eating, always have these great ingredients in your freezer ready to cook up. The more prepared you are, the less likely you will be to make poor choices nutritionally.

Make up a big batch of bone broth on the weekend and freeze it so that you can use it for quick and easy meals in months to come.

Give offal a try

Offal is very nutrient dense, meaning it offers you vitamins and minerals that other cuts of meat simply cannot match. By cooking with offal, you respect the animal from which it comes as you are using it completely, nose to tail, meaning there is no wastage. And that is better for you and the environment.

KICKSTART PLAN

The paleo lifestyle recalibrates your system in such a way that you eat only when you are hungry, stop eating when you are full and make smarter choices about how you nourish your body. Using the recipes in this book, I have put together a kickstart plan with five weeks of meal plans to help you achieve your wellness goals quickly, with ease and with noticeable long-term benefits. It takes around ten weeks to really see the full benefits of this way of eating, so you'll need to double the program. This program is sustainable in all senses of the word: you are fuelling your body with nutrient-dense foods and you are nurturing the environment by supporting sustainable farming, fishing and grazing practices.

So what changes will you notice? Well, within the first two weeks you should feel a difference in your energy levels and will be less likely to suffer from mid-afternoon slumps caused by sky-rocketing blood sugar. And when it comes to bedtime, you will sleep like a baby. It has been proven that it takes three weeks to create a habit, and I am happy to tell you that by the four-week mark the cravings for bad stuff, such as refined carbohydrates, sugar and stimulants, should be virtually gone. By the five-week mark, you will be burning excess body fat and gaining lean muscle mass. Ideally, at this stage, to see the maximum benefits, you should extend the program for another five weeks.

MAKE THE MOST OF LEFTOVERS

Leftovers make the perfect next-day breakfast or lunch. Instead of overeating 'just because they are there', pack whatever leftovers you have into storage containers to enjoy the next day. Not only does this minimise wastage, it also saves time.

At the important ten-week milestone, you will be aware of the major physical and mental changes that have occurred. You will feel like a new person. Your mental, emotional and psychological clarity will be unlike anything you've ever experienced and your outlook will be positive and focused. This is when you realise you have tightened and toned your way to good health, not only on the outside but on the inside as well. Embrace it!

Picture how wonderful it will be to bound out of bed with a positive mindset, heaps of energy and the type of focus that sees you tackle any of life's challenges your day throws at you. Positive energy attracts positive energy. If you put the right stuff out there, you will receive the right stuff back. Dare to make this a reality.

Snack time

I haven't included snacks in the meal plans that follow, but check out the snacks chapter, choose a few different things for the week and prepare them in bulk if possible so that you always have something at the ready for when hunger strikes or when friends pop in. Fermented veggies (see page 110, 116 and 121) and avocado are a great snack combination. They are nourishing for the gut and the good fats in the avocado give you a sustained release of energy. I also love beef jerky – just make sure you look for grass-fed, low-sodium options. It is easy to travel with and is so delicious.

Remember to be super organised. Make lists, keep a journal and keep on top of everything. If your fridge and pantry are filled with the right stuff, that will help you reach your goals. Minimise wastage by freezing foods and using leftovers. And it doesn't hurt to have some nutritious snacks in the fridge, handy for those times when you need to eat on the run.

So here you go, guys, our exciting journey together has begun. You have the power to turn this plan, this goal, into a tangible reality. Back yourself, love yourself and stick to it. I know you can do it. By creating a healthier you, you will encourage and become an inspiration to everyone around you. I cannot wait to see what an amazingly positive impact the paleo way will have, not only on you, but on the world. Keep cooking with love and laughter, every day.

EATING OUT

Sometimes it can be hard to make healthy choices when eating out or getting take-away. My advice is to keep it as clean as possible. Opt for dishes without dressings or sauces (or ask for the dressing on the side) so that you have more control over the amounts of salt and sugar that might have been added. Sashimi is a great option, as are grilled meats with vegetables on the side.

WEEK 1

FOCUS

It's your first week of transitioning to a paleo way of eating, and your focus should be on cooking up big batches of each dinner meal so that you have leftovers for lunch or snacks the next day – and perhaps even the day after! This style of cooking is key to the paleo lifestyle and will really help you to stay on track and not be tempted by unhealthy take-away options at lunch. Make every Sunday night 'roast night' and spend time with your family cooking up a beautiful piece of meat as well as a big batch of roast veggies that you can use for breakfasts and lunches later in the week. Do all of your shopping for ingredients on the weekend so that everything is ready to go. Please try to start serving each evening meal with some fermented veggies and a salad or vegetable side to really increase your vegetable intake. See the Salads and Vegetables chapter for loads of ideas.

	MONDAY	TUESDAY	WEDNESDAY
BREAKFAST	Paleo parfait with coconut cream (page 101)	Kale and pumpkin tortilla (page 102) using leftover roast veg	Healing chicken and vegetable soup leftove (page 156) with some eggs stirred through for added protein
LUNCH	Celery boats with herbed chicken salad (page 209) and Hard-boiled eggs (page 197)	Healing chicken and vegetable soup leftovers (page 156)	Bolognese on sautéec kale leftovers (page 18
DINNER	Healing chicken and vegetable soup (page 156)	Bolognese on sautéed kale (page 189)	Cauliflower fried rice with greens and sriracha (page 166)

Make up a double batch of chicken and vegetable soup (page 156) on Monday night so that you can enjoy the leftovers throughout the week.

These fish parcels (page 147) make the perfect Sunday lunch.

Cauliflower fried rice (page 166) is a fabulous and fast mid-week dinner.

THURSDAY	FRIDAY	SATURDAY	SUNDAY
Scrambled eggs with smoked trout and herbs (page 98)	Avocado, coconut and mint smoothie (page 230)	Miso soup with prawns (page 96)	Classic poached eggs with bacon, avocado and silverbeet (page 90)
Cauliflower fried rice with greens and sriracha leftovers (page 166)	Shepherd's pie leftovers (page 186)	Lamb meatballs with pumpkin and pomegranate (page 178)	Herb and garlic fish parcels (page 147)
Shepherd's pie (page 186) and Autumn greens with bacon, almond and paprika dressing (page 118)	Barbecued wild fish with smoky chorizo salad (page 190)	Barbecued sirloin with mushrooms, horseradish and rocket (page 190)	Roasted paprika chicken (page 165) and Roasted vegetables with mojo aioli (page 122)

WEEK 2

FOCUS

While following the paleo way, you can eat as many fibrous veggies as you like, and also as much good-quality fat as you need to satisfy your appetite. So let's focus this week on incorporating even more fresh, non-starchy vegetables into your diet. Serve every main meal with your choice of vegetable or salad dish (see pages 107–134). And if you feel hungry in between meals, snack on kale chips (see recipe, page 203), sticks of raw veg (carrot, cucumber, capsicum and celery are all great), or even a smoothie with heaps of leafy greens blended through it (see recipe, page 230). Add an extra spoonful of coconut oil to your smoothie to increase your good fats, or drizzle some extra-virgin olive oil over finished dishes recommended for this week such as pork stuffed mushrooms and Thai beef mince.

	MONDAY	TUESDAY	WEDNESDAY
BREAKFAST	Kale and pumpkin tortilla (page 102) using leftover roast meat and veg	Nic's paleo bread (page 200) with soft-boiled eggs and Kimchi (page 110)	Paleo parfait with coconut cream (page 101)
LUNCH	Roasted paprika chicken leftovers (page 165)	Chicken cacciatore leftovers (page 154)	Pork and garlic stuffed mushrooms leftovers (page 168)
DINNER	Chicken cacciatore (page 154) and Cauliflower rice (page 109)	Pork and garlic stuffed mushrooms (page 168) and Raw cauliflower tabouli (page 124)	Thai beef mince wit fried eggs (page 18 and Asian mushroo salad (page 130)

Make a loaf of Nic's paleo bread (page 200) on the weekend so that you can enjoy it for breakfasts and lunches throughout the week.

This tortilla recipe (page 102) is so versatile – you can basically add whatever veg and protein you have in the fridge.

I particularly love having Thai beef mince (page 180) for brekkie!

THURSDAY	FRIDAY	SATURDAY	SUNDAY
Thai beef mince leftovers (page 180) with some eggs cracked in and baked in the oven	Creamy chai smoothie (page 234)	Asian-style fried eggs with herbs and sriracha (page 95)	Chia seed congee with ginger and sesame (page 104) – you'll need to start this the night before
Salad sandwich with Nic's paleo bread (page 200), Hard-boiled eggs (page 197), avocado and loads of grated veg	Lamb moussaka leftovers (page 177)	Chilled avocado soup with poached prawns and mango (page 148)	Helen's creamy chicken and cabbage salad (page 153)
Lamb moussaka (page 177) and Moroccan carrot salad (page 133)	Vietnamese chicken wings (page 159) and Sautéed silverbeet with garlic and hazelnuts (page 134)	Chorizo and seafood 'paella' (page 141)	Spiced roast beef (page 192) and Sautéed kale with tahini and coconut dressing (page 122)

WEEK 3

FOCUS

You'll be getting into the swing of things by now and it's time to start thinking about incorporating more fermented foods into your diet. The good bacteria they contain is so great for our gut health, which in turn can affect so many aspects of our overall health. Of course, it takes some time for vegetables to ferment, around 10–14 days, so you'll need to prepare some in advance. I've included three delicious fermented veggie recipes in this book – kimchi (page 110), fermented vegetables with thyme (page 116) and sauerkraut with dill and juniper berries (page 121) – so have a look and see what takes your fancy. I suggest gradually incorporating them into your daily diet – starting with a teaspoon of fermented veg with every meal and working up to 1 tablespoon. Encourage your kids to have a try too and don't be discouraged if they turn up their noses. Just keep offering it every so often and one day they may decide they love it!

	MONDAY	TUESDAY	WEDNESDAY
BREAKFAST	Kale and pumpkin tortilla (page 102)	Broccoli 'rice' leftovers (page 109) sautéed with leftover roast veg and eggs	Paleo parfait with coconut cream (page 101)
LUNCH	Spiced roast beef leftovers (page 192)	Meatballs with tomato and bone marrow sauce leftovers (page 183)	Chicken liver curry leftovers (page 162)
DINNER	Meatballs with tomato and bone marrow sauce (page 183) and Broccoli 'rice' (page 109)	Chicken liver curry (page 162) with Cauliflower 'rice' (page 109)	Sashimi salad (page 144)

This Balinese roast pork belly (page 172) makes a pretty special Sunday roast!

Leftover broccoli rice (page 109) makes an awesome breakfast when sautéed with veg and eggs.

Add a little sauerkraut (page 121) or other fermented veg to every meal.

THURSDAY	FRIDAY	SATURDAY	SUNDAY
Chia seed congee with ginger and sesame (page 104) – you'll need to start this the night before	Scrambled eggs with smoked trout and herbs (page 98)	Classic poached eggs with bacon, avocado and silverbeet (page 90)	Chia and coconut custard (page 98) – you'll need to make this the night before
Macadamia cheese (page 206) with raw vegetable sticks, Hard-boiled eggs (page 197) and Spiced activated nuts and seeds (page 198)	Homemade merguez sausages leftovers (page 174) and Sauerkraut with dill and juniper berries (page 121)	Raw rainbow pad Thai (page 127)	Chopped chicken salad with bacon and sherry vinaigrette (page 160)
Homemade merguez sausages (page 174) and Moroccan carrot salad (page 133)	Sichuan chicken salad with egg 'noodles' (page 150)	Lemongrass prawn skewers (page 138) with a simple garden salad	Balinese roast pork belly (page 172) and steamed Asian greens

WEEK 4

FOCUS

Bone broths are so incredibly healing, especially for our gut and joints. They contain numerous minerals, such as magnesium and phosphorus, as well as glucosamine from the broken down cartilage and tendons. In preparation for this week, make up a big batch of your choice of bone broth on the weekend so that you can use it for quick and nutritious meals throughout the week. I've included recipes for beef, chicken and fish bone broths (pages 255–258) so take your pick, or maybe even choose a couple! Store your leftovers in the fridge or freezer. I've also included a couple of smoothies for breakfast this week as they are a great way to get a burst of protein, good fats and nutrients when you don't have much time in the morning. Of course, if time is not a problem, please feel free to make a luxurious poached egg breakfast with all the trimmings any morning of the week!

	MONDAY	TUESDAY	WEDNESDAY
BREAKFAST	Balinese roast pork belly leftovers (page 172) warmed with some veggies in bone broth (pages 255–258)	Creamy chai smoothie (page 234)	Eggs (however you lik them!) with Sautéed ka leftovers (page 122)
LUNCH	Tuna and bacon cucumber boats (page 215) with Spiced activated nuts and seeds (page 198) and Curried macadamia kale chips (page 203)	Cauliflower fried rice with greens and sriracha leftovers (page 166)	Pepper beef hotpot leftovers (page 184)
DINNER	Cauliflower fried rice with greens and sriracha (page 166) and Kimchi (page 110)	Pepper beef hotpot (page 184) and Sautéed kale with tahini and coconut dressing (page 122)	Pork cutlets with romesco sauce and cabbage slaw (page 171)

Smoothies are great for breakfast on the run!

Make up a big batch of nourishing bone broth (pages 255–258) to enjoy throughout the week.

These tuna cucumber boats (page 215) make a quick and easy lunch.

THURSDAY	FRIDAY	SATURDAY	SUNDAY
Asian-style fried eggs with herbs and sriracha (page 95)	Avocado, coconut and mint smoothie (page 230)	Classic poached eggs with bacon, avocado and silverbeet (page 90) – or use whichever trimmings you prefer!	Miso soup with prawns (page 96)
Bone broth (pages 255–258) warmed with eftover pork cutlet meat page 171) and veggies	Bolognese on sautéed kale leftovers (page 189)	Barbecued wild fish with smoky chorizo salad (page 142)	Raw cauliflower tabouli (page 124) and Moroccan carrot salad (page 133)
Bolognese on sautéed kale (page 189)	Vietnamese chicken wings (page 159) and Indian-spiced okra (page 115)	Herb and garlic fish parcels (page 147) and Sautéed silverbeet with garlic and hazelnuts (page 134)	Roasted paprika chicken (page 165) – or roast chicken any way you like it!

WEEK 5

FOCUS

You should be starting to get the hang of this style of cooking and eating by now and you may already be starting to notice some changes in your energy levels. However, the 10-week mark is when you will really start to see some significant changes in terms of your weight, mood, mental clarity and skin, so after you've finished Week 5, go back to Week 1 and repeat the program. After 10 weeks, any cravings will definitely have stopped and you will most likely be feeling so amazing that it will not be hard to stay motivated and continue on with this way of eating. This week, try to focus on drinking enough water. It seems like an obvious thing, but so many people don't have nearly enough. I start every day with a big glass of room-temperature water with either lemon juice or apple cider vinegar (page 220). Try making this part of your morning ritual too and see the different it makes.

	MONDAY	TUESDAY	WEDNESDAY
BREAKFAST	Roasted paprika chicken leftovers (page 165) fried up with some eggs and greens	Nic's paleo bread (page 200) with eggs any way you like them and Fermented vegetables with thyme (page 116)	Chia and coconut custard (page 92) – you'll need to make this the night before
LUNCH	Snags with sauerkraut and tomato ketchup (page 212)	Shepherd's pie leftovers (page 186)	Chicken cacciatore leftovers (page 154)
DINNER	Shepherd's pie (page 186) and Autumn greens with smoked paprika, bacon and almond dressing (page 118)	Chicken cacciatore (page 154) and Tomato and pomegranate chopped salad (page 128)	Meatballs with tomat and bone marrow sauce (page 183)

Start every day with a glass of room-temperature lemon water (page 220).

Sautéed kale (page 122) is one of my absolute favourite sides and goes with pretty much everything.

Snags with sauerkraut and homemade tomato ketchup (page 212) – such a beautifully simple lunch.

THURSDAY	FRIDAY	SATURDAY	SUNDAY
Asian-style fried eggs with herbs and sriracha (page 95)	Avocado, coconut and mint smoothie (page 230)	Scrambled eggs with smoked trout and herbs (page 98)	Paleo parfait with coconut cream (page 101)
Meatballs with tomato nd bone marrow sauce leftovers (page 183)	Healing chicken and vegetable soup leftovers (page 156)	Sichuan chicken salad with egg 'noodles' (page 150)	Sashimi salad (page 144)
Healing chicken and vegetable soup (page 156)	Pork and garlic stuffed mushrooms (page 168) and Sautéed kale with tahini and coconut dressing (page 122)	Homemade merguez sausages (page 174) and Raw cauliflower tabouli (page 124)	Roast pork, beef, chicken – whatever takes your fancy – and your pick of a veggie side (pages 165, 172 or 192)

Recipes

COOK
with
Himalayan
Salt

BREAKFASTS

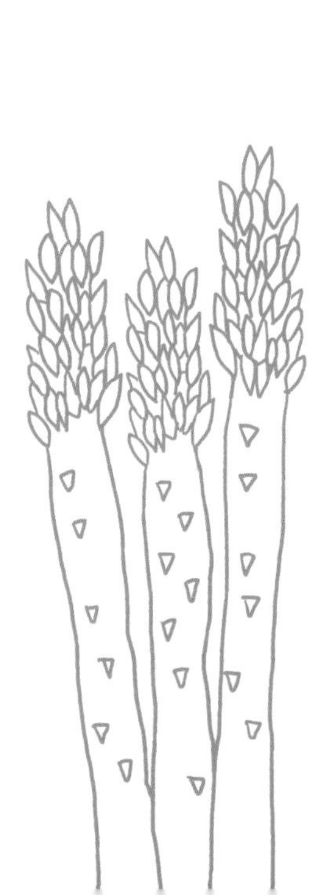

Classic poached eggs with bacon, avocado and silverbeet

Eggs are an awesome way to get some good fats into your system, which will keep you full for longer. I love to team my eggs with vibrant greens; in this instance I've used silverbeet, but you could also use broccoli, kale, okra or asparagus. Try to find bacon from free-range pigs if possible, but if you can't simply add some meat from last night's dinner, such as roast chicken or prawns, instead. I also love to add some fermented vegetables (see recipe, page 116) to the side of this dish – not only do they taste great, they also help to break down the protein and add beneficial bacteria to your stomach.

- 2 tablespoons apple cider vinegar
- 4 eggs
- 1 tablespoon coconut oil or other good-quality fat*
- 8 slices of bacon
- 2 garlic cloves, thinly sliced
- 2 silverbeet leaves (stalks removed and reserved for making bone broths), roughly chopped
- sea salt and freshly ground black pepper
- 1 avocado, sliced
- 1 tablespoon chopped flat-leaf parsley leaves, to serve (optional)
- Nic's Paleo Bread (see recipe, page 200), to serve (optional)

** See Setting Up Your Paleo Kitchen*

To poach the eggs, pour the vinegar into a saucepan of boiling salted water, then reduce the heat to medium–low so the water is just simmering. Crack an egg into a cup. Using a wooden spoon, stir the simmering water in one direction to form a whirlpool and drop the egg into the centre. Repeat with the remaining eggs and cook for 3 minutes, or until the eggs are cooked to your liking. Use a slotted spoon to remove the eggs, then place them on some paper towel to soak up the excess water.

Heat a touch of the oil or fat in a non-stick frying pan over medium–high heat. Add the bacon and fry for 3 minutes on each side until slightly coloured (cook for longer if you like it crispy). Remove from the pan, drain on paper towel and keep warm.

To finish, heat a touch more oil or fat in the pan, add the garlic and cook until fragrant, about 30 seconds. Stir in the silverbeet and cook until the silverbeet is wilted, 1–2 minutes. Season with salt and pepper.

To serve, divide the silverbeet among four warm serving plates, then top with two slices of bacon and a poached egg. Divide the avocado slices among the plates and sprinkle on some salt, pepper and chopped parsley (if using). Serve with paleo bread, if you like.

SERVES 4

Chia and coconut custard

My wife, Nic, makes the best chia seed breakfasts and this is no exception. I hope it becomes one of your favourites! The addition of raw egg is what really excites me about this recipe, but just make sure you source the best quality eggs possible, from pasture-raised chickens. This is a great recipe to experiment with – try using different spices, such as cardamom, turmeric or nutmeg, and different nuts to sprinkle on top. You could also add slippery elm, pau d'arco or licorice root powder for an extra nutritional boost.

- 70 g (⅓ cup) white or black chia seeds
- 250 ml (1 cup) coconut water
- 250 ml (1 cup) coconut milk
- 2 eggs
- 1 tablespoon coconut oil
- 1 vanilla bean, split and seeds scraped
- 1 teaspoon ground cinnamon
- pinch of Himalayan or sea salt
- mixed berries, to serve
- chopped almonds (activated if possible, see page 198), to serve

Combine the chia seeds and coconut water in a large bowl. Set aside.

Pour the coconut milk into a saucepan and bring to a simmer over medium–low heat. Add the eggs, coconut oil, vanilla, cinnamon and salt and whisk for 3 minutes, until slightly thickened.

Add the egg and coconut milk mix to the bowl with the chia seeds and stir well.

Pour into 3–4 small bowls, depending on how generous you'd like the servings to be. Place the bowls in the fridge for at least 1 hour, or overnight, to set.

To serve, simply top with some fresh berries and almonds.

SERVES 3–4

Tip

If you are not able to eat eggs, simply omit them from the recipe – it will still be delicious and nourishing.

Asian-style fried eggs with herbs and sriracha

I adore the flavours that Asian herbs, spices and sauces bring to this dish. If you're feeling adventurous, look for duck eggs at your butcher – they taste richer than chicken eggs and have more omega-3 fatty acids. This recipe also makes a great lunch or dinner, especially if you're short on time. I like to add heaps of chopped carrot, sprouts, steamed broccoli or cauliflower and some rocket or lettuce leaves to make a simple egg salad. Stir through a bit of mayo (see recipe, page 250) and you've got the perfect mid-week meal.

- 100 ml coconut oil or other good-quality fat*
- 4 eggs
- sea salt and freshly ground black pepper
- 1–2 tablespoons Paleo Sriracha Chilli Sauce (see recipe, page 249), or to taste
- 2 handfuls of mixed herbs (such as mint, coriander and Thai basil leaves)
- 1 long red chilli, finely sliced
- 1 spring onion, finely sliced
- 1 teaspoon black and white sesame seeds, toasted

Tamari dressing

- ½ teaspoon finely grated ginger
- 1 garlic clove, finely grated
- 1½ teaspoons tamari or coconut aminos*
- 1 teaspoon apple cider vinegar
- ½ teaspoon sesame oil
- 1 tablespoon water

** See Setting Up Your Paleo Kitchen*

To make the tamari dressing, combine all the ingredients in a small bowl and mix well. Set aside.

Heat the oil or fat in a wok or large frying pan over high heat until nice and hot. Crack the eggs, one at a time, into a small bowl and then drop each egg into the hot oil. (You may need to do this in two batches.) Cook the eggs for 20 seconds, then flip over. Reduce the heat to medium and cook for a further 30 seconds until they are nice and crisp. The yolk should be still runny at this point. Remove the eggs with a slotted spoon and place on some paper towel to soak up any excess oil. Carefully pour the hot oil or fat out of the pan and reserve for another use.

Season the eggs with salt and pepper, then drizzle on some tamari dressing and sriracha (add more sriracha if you like it hot). Garnish each plate with a handful of herbs, then sprinkle on some chilli, spring onion and sesame seeds.

SERVES 2

Tip

If you can't tolerate eggs, try replacing them with a few fillets of fish and reducing the amount of oil used to cook them. Any kind of wild, line-caught fish will go beautifully with these herbs and dressing.

Miso soup with prawns

I have included this recipe as I absolutely love having soups for breakfast. If you are avoiding soy products then just leave out the miso and pop some bonito flakes and extra seaweed in there. If you do include the miso, make sure you source an organic, non-GMO, fermented option. It's important to use a homemade bone broth to maximise the flavour and nutrients. You can add an egg or two to this soup to make it even more filling. And a final tip: purchase a few good-quality thermoses so that you can pack this soup for yourself and your kids for lunch.

- 1 litre (4 cups) Fish Bone Broth or Chicken Bone Broth (see recipes, pages 255 and 256)
- 2 teaspoons dried wakame (see note)
- 150 g kelp noodles (see note)
- 200 g cauliflower, roughly chopped into florets
- 6 shiitake mushrooms, sliced
- 100 g daikon*, peeled and cut into 1-cm pieces
- 3 spring onions, finely sliced
- 8 fresh okra pods*, chopped
- 8 raw king prawns, shelled and deveined with tails intact
- 125 ml (½ cup) miso paste

To serve

- toasted sesame seeds (optional)
- sesame oil
- dried chilli flakes (optional)
- bonito flakes (see note)

** See Setting Up Your Paleo Kitchen*

Note

Wakame, a type of seaweed, is available from Asian grocers, health food stores and some supermarkets. Bonito flakes are made from fermented bonito fish and can be found at Asian grocers. Kelp noodles are made from seaweed and are available from health food stores.

Bring the bone broth to the boil in a large saucepan over medium heat, add the wakame and simmer for 20 minutes, or until the wakame has expanded. Add the kelp noodles and vegetables and cook for 5 minutes, then add the prawns and cook for a further 2 minutes, or until the prawns are almost cooked through and the vegetables are tender. Add the miso – the best way to do this is to push it through a strainer into the pan (this evenly distributes it in the stock). When the miso has dissolved, after about 1–2 minutes (stir gently if you need to), the soup is ready.

To serve, spoon the soup into four warm serving bowls. Scatter over some sesame seeds (if using) and sprinkle on 1–2 drops of sesame oil, some chilli flakes (if using) and some bonito flakes.

SERVES 4

Scrambled eggs with smoked trout and herbs

These eggs are super easy and will take no more than 10 minutes to get from the fridge to your breakfast plate. I urge you to spend your money on the best possible eggs you can find. Most free-range eggs are a far cry from what you would think – free-range could just mean that the chickens have an A4-sized piece of land for themselves and the ground is dirt. I always look for pasture-raised, organic eggs to ensure that the chickens have the ability to peck for insects and to eat a balanced diet. This in turn produces the most nutritious eggs for us to consume. You can omit the fish from this dish or replace it with some sautéed greens. Sprinkle on some toasted sesame seeds or roasted activated nuts, or even fold in some of last night's leftover bolognese sauce (see recipe, page 189).

4 eggs

2 tablespoons coconut cream

2 chives, finely chopped

sea salt and freshly ground black pepper

1 tablespoon coconut oil or other good-quality fat*

240 g smoked trout, flaked

Herb salad

3 radishes, thinly sliced

2 marinated artichokes, flaked

2 handfuls of mixed herbs (tarragon, chives, dill, flat-leaf parsley, watercress, celery leaves)

Mustard Vinaigrette (see recipe, page 238)

To serve

1½ tablespoons salmon roe

½ teaspoon grated fresh horseradish

lemon wedges (optional)

Nic's Paleo Bread (see recipe, page 200) (optional)

** See Setting Up Your Paleo Kitchen*

To make the herb salad, gently toss the radish, artichoke and herbs in a small bowl with the vinaigrette.

Whisk the eggs, coconut cream and chives in a bowl and season with salt and pepper.

Melt the oil or fat in a non-stick frying pan over medium heat, pour in the egg mixture and stir gently with a wooden spoon until the eggs set, 2–3 minutes.

Divide the eggs between two plates and top with the trout and herb salad. Scatter over the salmon roe and horseradish. Serve with the lemon wedges and paleo bread (if using).

SERVES 2

Paleo parfait with coconut cream

I wish I could take the credit for this awesome dish, but it was created by my dear friend and fitness guru Luke Hines, who is truly passionate about food and nutrition. This recipe was first published in Luke's book with Scott Gooding, *Clean Living*. Make a big jar of the paleo muesli and keep it in the fridge so that you can have brekkie on the table in less than 5 minutes! I don't recommend eating this more than once a week if you're on my kickstart program (see page 74), as the honey in it can cause sweet cravings.

- 1 × 400 ml can coconut cream, unopened can chilled overnight in the fridge
- 1 tablespoon honey (optional)
- 230 g (1½ cups) frozen mixed berries
- 1 apple, grated
- 1 large carrot, grated
- 4 tablespoons goji berries (see note), soaked in 125 ml (½ cup) water for 10 minutes, then drained

Paleo muesli

- 80 g (½ cup) flaxseeds (linseeds)*
- 3 tablespoons pumpkin seeds (activated if possible, see page 198)
- 3 tablespoons sesame seeds
- 80 g (½ cup) almonds (activated if possible, see page 198)
- 55 g (scant 1 cup) shredded coconut

To serve

- cacao nibs (see note)
- fresh berries
- baby mint leaves

* *See Setting Up Your Paleo Kitchen*

Note

Cacao nibs are made from cacao beans that have been roasted, de-husked and chopped. Goji berries are native to China and are bright pink with a sweet and sour flavour. Both are available from health food stores.

To make the muesli, preheat the oven to 180°C. Line three baking trays with baking paper. On one baking tray, toast the flaxseeds, pumpkin seeds and sesame seeds for 8–10 minutes until golden. On the second baking tray, toast the almonds for 8–10 minutes until lightly coloured. On the third baking tray, toast the coconut for 2–3 minutes, or until lightly golden. Once the ingredients are toasted, roughly chop the almonds, combine them with the seeds in a large bowl and set aside to cool.

Meanwhile, remove the chilled can of coconut cream from the fridge, open and scoop out the contents into another bowl. Separate the hardened cream layer from the water layer. Place the cream layer and ½ tablespoon of honey (if using) in a bowl and beat with an electric mixer for about 5 minutes on high speed, until soft peaks form. Refrigerate until ready to serve. The water layer can be reserved for using in smoothies.

Combine the frozen berries and the remaining honey (if using) in a saucepan and slowly cook over low–medium heat until they reach a sauce-like consistency, about 5–10 minutes. Mash the berries up to create a puree, then set aside.

Combine the apple, carrot and goji berries with the muesli and set aside.

Spoon a couple of tablespoons of the muesli mixture into a glass, then add a couple of dollops of coconut cream, then some berry puree. Continue layering in the same order until you fill the glass. Repeat to fill three more glasses. If you like, finish with a sprinkle of cacao nibs, fresh berries and mint leaves.

SERVES 4

Kale and pumpkin tortilla

This is a delicious and simple breakfast dish that is also perfect for taking to work or packing in your kids' lunchboxes. If you don't have any kale, you can pretty much use any kind of cooked veggies or meat instead – simply pop your leftover roast veg or meat from the night before into the pan, add some eggs and *voila*! Breakfast has never been so tasty or quick and there is no waste.

¼ bunch of kale leaves (about 100 g), central stalks removed

6 eggs

sea salt and freshly ground black pepper

2 tablespoons coconut oil or other good-quality fat *

100 g pumpkin, cut into 1-cm cubes

1 garlic clove, crushed

2 tablespoons sunflower seeds (activated if possible, see page 198)

2 tablespoons pumpkin seeds (activated if possible, see page 198)

lemon wedges, to serve

** See Setting Up Your Paleo Kitchen*

Wash the kale leaves thoroughly to remove any grit. Drain well, pat dry and roughly chop. Set aside.

Using a fork, lightly beat the eggs in a bowl and season with salt and pepper.

Heat the oil or fat in a non-stick frying pan over medium heat. Add the pumpkin and cook, stirring occasionally, for 3 minutes. Reduce the heat to medium–low, add the garlic and cook for a further 2 minutes, or until the pumpkin is softened. Increase the heat to medium, add the kale and cook, stirring constantly, for 1 minute. Spread out the kale and pumpkin into a single layer and pour in the beaten egg, swirling the egg around the pan. Reduce the heat to low and cook, without stirring, for 2–3 minutes, or until the egg is almost cooked through. Take off the heat, cover with a lid and leave for 3 minutes to allow the residual heat in the pan to finish cooking the tortilla.

Cut the tortilla in half, then gently slide each half onto a warm plate. Sprinkle on some sunflower and pumpkin seeds and squeeze on a little lemon juice.

SERVES 2

Chia seed congee with ginger and sesame

This is a healthier take on the traditional congee, which is a starchy, rice-based porridge with little nutritional value. I wanted to create a protein-packed, nutrient-dense dish, so have used chia seeds instead of white rice. It's vital to use homemade chicken or beef bone broth in this dish for the best nutritional value and also flavour. A tablespoon of kimchi (see recipe, page 110) is fabulous with this congee as the spices work beautifully together. Double the quantity of this recipe and you will have leftovers to enjoy for lunch or dinner, or a great snack for the kids when they get home from school. You will need to start this recipe the night before.

150 g chia seeds

2.5-cm piece of ginger, finely grated

1 litre (4 cups) Chicken Bone Broth or Beef Bone Broth (see recipes, pages 256 and 258)

1 tablespoon coconut oil or other good-quality fat*

2 slices of bacon, chopped into large pieces

1 handful of coriander leaves, roughly chopped

2 spring onions, white and green parts, finely sliced

2 long red chillies, finely sliced

2 tablespoons tamari

sea salt and freshly ground white pepper

4 eggs

To serve

toasted sesame seeds

coriander leaves

sesame oil

Kimchi (see recipe, page 110)

** See Setting Up Your Paleo Kitchen*

Place the chia seeds, ginger and bone broth in a container, cover and store in the refrigerator overnight.

The next morning, pour the chia mixture and 250 ml of water (or bone broth if you have some handy) into a large saucepan and bring to the boil. Reduce the heat to low and simmer for 5 minutes, stirring occasionally, until lovely and soupy.

Meanwhile, heat the coconut oil or fat in a frying pan over medium heat, add the bacon and fry until it just starts to become crisp, then remove and set aside.

Add the bacon, chopped coriander, spring onion, chilli and tamari to the chia mixture. Season with salt and pepper and simmer for 2 minutes. Divide the congee between four serving bowls, make a well in the centre and crack an egg into each one. Allow to stand for 3–5 minutes so the heat from the congee cooks the egg. Sprinkle with the sesame seeds and coriander leaves, drizzle with the sesame oil and serve with the kimchi.

SERVES 4

CULTURE
FOR LIFE
pete evans

SALADS & VEGETABLES

Broccoli 'rice'

You might have noticed the craze over the last few years for cauliflower 'rice', made by blending cauliflower until it resembles rice. Well – wait for it – you can do the same thing with broccoli! It makes for a great side dish, is so much healthier than actual rice and is ready in just a few minutes. Something else I've been doing recently is holding a head of broccoli above my pot of soup, curry or sauce and simply running a sharp knife over the broccoli so that all the tiny pieces fall into the pot. The remaining stalk can then be chopped and used for a stock or soup, or you can even use a mandoline slicer to create broccoli 'noodles'!

- 2 heads of broccoli (about 400 g each), roughly chopped into florets
- 2 tablespoons coconut oil or other good-quality fat*
- sea salt and freshly ground black pepper

** See Setting Up Your Paleo Kitchen*

Simply place the broccoli in the bowl of a food processor and pulse into tiny, fine pieces that look like rice.

Heat the oil or fat in a frying pan over medium heat, add the broccoli and cook, stirring occasionally, for 4–5 minutes, or until softened. Season with salt and pepper and serve. It is perfect with any kind of stew, stir-fry or curry – see the main meals chapter for some ideas.

SERVES 4–6

Cauliflower 'rice'

To make cauliflower rice instead, simply replace the 2 heads of broccoli with 1 large head of cauliflower and follow the same method. Cauliflower rice is delicious used in fried rice (see recipe, page 166) or to make a grain-free tabouli (see recipe, page 124).

Kimchi

Kimchi is Korean fermented cabbage and I am hoping this kick-ass dish becomes a staple in your home alongside the other fermented vegetables you make. Whenever we are cooking an Asian-inspired dish at home, such as eggs, curry, stir-fry, salad or even some satay sticks on the barbecue, we bring out the kimchi to serve alongside it. Play around with the spices and simply reduce the amount of chilli if you don't like it super hot.

- ½ Chinese cabbage (wong bok) (about 500 g)
- 3 radishes or 1 daikon*
- 1–2 carrots
- 1–2 onions
- 1½ teaspoons sea salt
- 3–4 garlic cloves, finely sliced
- 3 tablespoons grated ginger
- 3–4 long red chillies, deseeded and finely sliced
- 2 large handfuls of coriander roots, stems and leaves, finely chopped
- 1 tablespoon Korean chilli powder (gochugaru) (see note) (optional)
- 1 teaspoon ground turmeric (optional)
- 1 sachet vegetable starter culture (this will weigh 2–5 g, depending on the brand) (see note)

** See Setting Up Your Paleo Kitchen*

Note

Available from Asian grocers, Korean chilli powder has smoky, fruity sweet notes and a hot kick. Vegetable starter culture can be used to kick-start the fermentation process when culturing veggies and is available from health food stores or online.

You will need a 1.5-litre preserving jar with an airlock lid for this recipe. Wash the jar and the utensils you will be using thoroughly in hot water or run them through a hot rinse cycle in the dishwasher.

Remove the outer leaves of the cabbage. Choose one, wash it well and set aside. Finely shred the cabbage, radishes or daikon, carrots and onions in the bowl of a food processor. (You can also use a mandoline or sharp knife to chop them finely.) In a large glass or stainless steel bowl, combine the cabbage with the radish or daikon, carrot and onion. Sprinkle on the salt and mix well. Add the garlic, ginger, chilli, coriander, chilli powder and turmeric (if using). Mix well, cover and set aside.

Dissolve the starter culture in water according to the packet instructions (the amount of water will depend on the brand). Add to the vegetables and mix well. Fill the prepared jar with the vegetable mixture, pressing down well with a large spoon or potato masher to remove any air pockets. Leave 2 cm of room free at the top. The vegetables should be completely submerged in the liquid, so add more water if necessary.

Fold the clean cabbage leaf, place it on top of the vegetable mixture and add a small glass weight (a shot glass is ideal) to keep everything submerged. Close the lid, then wrap a tea towel around the side of the jar to block out the light. Store in a dark place with a temperature of 16–23°C for 10–14 days. (You can place the jar in an esky to maintain a more consistent temperature.) Different vegetables have different culturing times and the warmer it is the shorter the time needed. The longer you leave the jar, the higher the level of good bacteria present and the tangier the flavour.

Chill before eating. Once opened, the kimchi will last for up to 2 months in the fridge when kept submerged in the liquid. If unopened, it will keep for up to 9 months in the fridge.

MAKES 1 × 1.5-LITRE JAR

Roasted vegetables with mojo aioli

This is a cracker of a recipe, full of flavour, colour, aroma and texture. The mojo aioli is inspired by mojo rojo, a chilli sauce that originated in the Canary Islands. Double this recipe so that you can take it to work the next day or turn it into a delicious egg bake for breakfast.

- 4 baby golden beetroot
- 4 baby red beetroot
- 80 ml (⅓ cup) coconut oil, melted
- sea salt and freshly ground black pepper
- 2 parsnips, halved lengthways and cut into 5-cm pieces
- 1 red onion, quartered
- 1 turnip, cut into quarters
- ¼ pumpkin, cut into wedges
- 200 g sweet potato, cut into wedges
- 2 carrots, halved lengthways and cut into 5-cm pieces
- 1 garlic bulb, cloves separated
- 1 teaspoon Jerk Spice Blend (see below), or more to taste
- 1 handful of coriander leaves

Jerk spice blend

- 1 tablespoon garlic powder
- 1 teaspoon cayenne pepper
- 2 teaspoons onion powder
- 2 teaspoons dried thyme
- 2 teaspoons dried parsley
- 1½ teaspoons paprika
- 1 teaspoon ground allspice
- ½ teaspoon freshly ground black pepper
- ½ teaspoon dried chilli flakes
- ½ teaspoon ground nutmeg
- ¼ teaspoon ground cinnamon
- 2 teaspoons sea salt

Mojo aioli

- 6 garlic cloves, chopped
- 1 teaspoon cumin seeds, toasted
- 2 long red chillies, deseeded and chopped
- 2 teaspoons smoked paprika
- ½ teaspoon dried oregano
- 2 tablespoons apple cider vinegar
- 3 tablespoons extra-virgin olive oil
- 4–6 tablespoons Aioli (see recipe, page 250)
- sea salt and freshly ground black pepper

To make the jerk spice blend, combine all the ingredients. (Leftover spice mix can be stored in an airtight container for up to 3 months.)

To make the mojo aioli, place the garlic, cumin and chilli in a food processor and process to form a paste. Add the paprika, oregano and vinegar, then slowly add the oil and process to form a thick paste. Mix with the aioli, adding more aioli if necessary, and season to taste. Refrigerate until ready to serve.

Preheat the oven to 200°C.

Wash the beetroot and trim the stems, leaving 1 cm intact. Place in a large roasting tin, drizzle over 1 teaspoon of the oil and season. Cover the tin with foil and roast for 40 minutes, shaking the tin after 20 minutes, until tender. When the beetroot is cool enough to touch, peel and halve.

Combine the vegetables and beetroot in the tin, toss with the remaining oil and sprinkle over the jerk spice mix. Spread the vegetables out to form a single layer and roast until tender and golden, about 30–35 minutes. Arrange on a platter, garnish with the coriander and serve with the mojo aioli.

SERVES 4–6

Indian-spiced okra

My favourite fruit in the world has to be okra! So what if it's a fruit that grows on a vegetable plant – it is bloody delicious and so good for you. Okra is mucilaginous, which means that it becomes slimy when you cook it and helps to thicken soups and sauces. It contains heaps of fibre, which is awesome for the health of your gut, as well as good levels of vitamin C, folate and antioxidants. We use it in lots of different ways at home – raw in salads, cooked into curries, stews and soups, tossed in the pan with some bacon and eggs in the morning, or cooked with fragrant spices as in this recipe and served as a side dish. You'll find okra at Asian grocers and some greengrocers.

- 3 tablespoons coconut oil or other good-quality fat*
- 2 teaspoons brown mustard seeds
- 14 fresh curry leaves
- ¼ onion, finely diced
- 1½ teaspoons ground cumin
- 1 teaspoon ground coriander
- 1½ teaspoons garam masala
- 2 teaspoons ground turmeric
- 1–2 long red chillies, thinly sliced diagonally
- 4 garlic cloves, crushed
- 600 g fresh okra pods*, cut in half diagonally
- sea salt and freshly ground black pepper

** See Setting Up Your Paleo Kitchen*

Heat the oil or fat in a wok or large frying pan over medium heat. Add the mustard seeds and cook until they start to pop, then add the curry leaves and fry for 20 seconds, or until they start to crisp. Stir in the onion and continue to cook, stirring occasionally, for a further 2 minutes until it begins to caramelise slightly.

Add the ground spices to the pan and cook, stirring constantly, for 1 minute until fragrant. Add the chilli, garlic and okra and give the pan a good shake, then add 125 ml of water and cook for 10 minutes, or until the okra is soft. Season with salt and pepper and serve.

SERVES 4

Fermented vegetables with thyme

I cannot emphasise enough how beneficial adding fermented vegetables into your daily diet can be, as long as your body can tolerate them. Scientists are now starting to realise how important our gut bacteria are, and fermented vegetables are a fabulous way of increasing your good bacteria.

- 2 teaspoons black peppercorns
- 2 whole cloves
- 3 baby golden beetroot, finely sliced into rounds using a mandoline
- 4 Dutch carrots, cut in half lengthways
- 4 radishes, cut in half lengthways
- 1 zucchini, sliced
- ½ red onion, sliced
- 2 garlic cloves, sliced
- 1 baby fennel bulb, finely sliced lengthways using a mandoline
- 6 brussels sprouts, cut in half
- 5-cm piece of fresh turmeric, peeled and finely sliced (optional)
- 2 teaspoons sea salt
- 1 sachet vegetable starter culture (this will weigh 2–5 g, depending on the brand) (see note)
- 3 thyme sprigs
- 2 bay leaves
- 1 small cabbage leaf, washed

Note

Vegetable starter culture can be used to kickstart the fermentation process when culturing veggies and is available from health food stores or online.

You will need a 1.5-litre preserving jar with an airlock lid for this recipe. Wash the jar and the utensils you will be using thoroughly in hot water or run them through a hot rinse cycle in the dishwasher.

Place the peppercorns and cloves in a small piece of muslin, tie into a bundle with kitchen string and set aside.

Place the vegetables and turmeric (if using) in a large glass or stainless steel bowl and sprinkle with salt. Mix, cover and set aside.

Dissolve the starter culture in water according to the packet instructions (the amount of water will depend on the brand you are using). Add to the vegetables along with the muslin bag containing the peppercorns and cloves, the thyme and bay leaves. Mix well.

Fill the prepared jar with the vegetables, pressing down well with a large spoon to remove any air pockets and leaving 2 cm of room free at the top. The vegetables should be completely submerged in the liquid, so add more water if necessary. Take the clean cabbage leaf, fold it up and place it on top of the vegetables, then add a small glass weight (a shot glass is ideal) to keep everything submerged. Close the lid, then wrap a tea towel around the side of the jar to block out the light. Store in a dark place with a temperature of 16–23°C for 10–14 days. (You can place the jar in an esky to maintain a more consistent temperature.) Different vegetables have different culturing times and the warmer it is the shorter the time needed. The longer you leave the jar, the higher the level of good bacteria present. It is up to you how long you leave it – some people prefer the tangier flavour that comes with extra fermenting time, while others prefer a milder flavour.

Chill before eating. Once opened, the vegetables will last for up to 2 months in the fridge when kept submerged in liquid. If unopened, they will keep for up to 9 months in the fridge.

MAKES 1 × 1.5-LITRE JAR

Autumn greens with bacon, almond and paprika dressing

I read a comment on my Facebook page recently that made me laugh: 'Just add bacon and it'll taste great!'. Bacon does make everything taste better. Superstar chef Heston Blumenthal has even made bacon ice cream ... though I think I'll pass on that one. Use whatever greens you have, or replace the greens with brussels sprouts, cauliflower, parsnips, carrots, okra, asparagus – in fact, pretty much any vegetable will work well. This might just be the dish that gets your children eating more greens!

- 2 tablespoons coconut oil
- 3 garlic cloves, crushed
- 500 g cavolo nero (Tuscan cabbage/kale), roughly chopped
- 6 silverbeet leaves, roughly chopped
- 1 tablespoon lemon juice, or to taste

Bacon, almond and paprika dressing

- 1 French shallot, finely chopped
- 1 tablespoon coconut oil
- 100 g bacon, finely diced
- 3 tablespoons sherry vinegar or apple cider vinegar
- 100 g almonds (activated if possible, see page 198), toasted and chopped
- 1 teaspoon finely snipped chives
- ½ teaspoon smoked paprika
- 100 ml extra-virgin olive oil
- sea salt and freshly ground black pepper

To make the dressing, in a small saucepan over low heat, gently cook the shallot in half of the coconut oil until soft, about 5 minutes. Remove from the pan, place in a bowl and set aside. Wipe the pan dry with paper towel, then place over medium heat. Add the remaining coconut oil and the bacon and fry, stirring occasionally, for 6–8 minutes, or until the bacon is crispy and golden. Stir in the vinegar and shallot and allow to cool. Transfer to a bowl and mix in the almonds, chives, paprika and olive oil and season with salt and pepper. Set aside until needed.

Melt the coconut oil in a frying pan over medium–high heat, add the garlic and cook for 30 seconds, or until softened and fragrant. Stir in the cavolo nero and silverbeet and sauté until wilted, about 2–3 minutes. Add a splash of water, then season with salt and pepper. Transfer to a large bowl, add half the dressing and toss well. Arrange the greens on a platter and drizzle with some lemon juice and some more dressing, if desired. This dish makes a great accompaniment to shepherd's pie (see recipe, page 186) or moussaka (see recipe, page 177).

SERVES 4

Sauerkraut with dill and juniper berries

In my perfect world, people would give jars of homemade sauerkraut as a gift for birthdays, Christmas and Valentine's Day instead of boxes of sugar-laden chocolates! Real fermented sauerkraut (not the stuff on the supermarket shelf that isn't refrigerated) is the simplest and most effective way to create good gut health. On top of that, fermented veggies are dirt cheap to make and absolutely delicious.

- 1 star anise
- 1 teaspoon whole cloves
- 600 g cabbage (you can use savoy or red, or a mixture of the two)
- 1½ teaspoons sea salt
- 3 tablespoons chopped dill
- 2 tablespoons juniper berries (see note)
- 1 sachet vegetable starter culture (this will weigh 2–5 g, depending on the brand) (see note)
- 1 handful of dill tips, to serve

Note

Juniper berries are purple in colour and are most famous for lending their flavour to gin. They can be found at some health food stores, specialty food stores or online. Vegetable starter culture can be used to kick-start the fermentation process when culturing veggies and is available from health food stores or online.

You will need a 1.5-litre preserving jar with an airlock lid for this recipe. Wash the jar and all the utensils you will be using in hot water or run them through a hot rinse cycle in the dishwasher.

Place the star anise and cloves in a small piece of muslin, tie into a bundle and set aside. Remove the outer leaves of the cabbage. Choose one of the outer leaves, wash it well and set aside. Shred the cabbage in a food processor, or slice by hand or use a mandoline, then place in a large glass or stainless steel bowl. Sprinkle on the salt, chopped dill and juniper berries, mix well, cover and set aside while you prepare the starter culture.

Dissolve the starter culture in water according to the packet instructions (the amount of water will depend on the brand you are using). Add to the cabbage along with the muslin bag containing the spices and mix well.

Fill the prepared jar with the cabbage, pressing down well with a large spoon or potato masher to remove any air pockets and leaving 2 cm of room free at the top. The cabbage should be completely submerged in the liquid; add more water if necessary.

Take the clean cabbage leaf, fold it up and place it on top of the cabbage mixture, then add a small glass weight (a shot glass is ideal) to keep everything submerged. Close the lid, then wrap a tea towel around the side of the jar to block out the light. Store in a dark place with a temperature of 16–23°C for 10–14 days. (Place the jar in an esky to maintain a more consistent temperature.) Different vegetables have different culturing times and the warmer it is the shorter the time needed. The longer you leave the jar, the higher the level of good bacteria present and the tangier the flavour.

Chill before eating. Once opened, mix through the dill tips and serve. The sauerkraut will last for up to 2 months in the fridge when kept submerged in the liquid. If unopened, it will keep for up to 9 months in the fridge.

MAKES 1 × 1.5-LITRE JAR

Sautéed kale with tahini and coconut dressing

Tahini is a paste made of crushed sesame seeds. It is great in bliss balls, smoothies, sauces and salad dressings like this one. To make this dish even quicker, you could replace the sautéed kale with some lettuce or rocket leaves and just drizzle this amazing dressing over the top. It also goes beautifully with any sautéed greens or roasted vegetables.

- 2 tablespoons coconut oil or other good-quality fat*
- 3 garlic cloves, crushed
- 1½ bunches of kale (about 600 g), central stalks removed and leaves torn
- 3 tablespoons pine nuts, toasted, plus extra to serve
- dried chilli flakes (optional)

Coconut yoghurt

- flesh and water of 4 young coconuts*
- juice of 2 lemons or limes
- 2 probiotic capsules (see note)

Tahini and coconut dressing

- 3 tablespoons hulled tahini
- 2 tablespoons lemon juice
- 1 garlic clove, crushed
- pinch of sea salt and freshly ground black pepper

** See Setting Up Your Paleo Kitchen*

Note

Probiotic capsules contain live bacteria that can help to improve the health of your gut. They are available at health food stores and pharmacies and must be kept in the fridge.

To make the coconut yoghurt, combine the coconut flesh, one-third of the coconut water and the lemon or lime juice. Blend until smooth and creamy. Depending on the consistency you prefer, you can add more coconut water. Open the probiotic capsules, tip the contents into the blender and give one final quick whiz. Pour into a 1-litre glass jar, cover with paper towel and allow to sit for 6–12 hours at room temperature so that the bacteria can proliferate (break down the yoghurt). The longer you leave it, the tangier the yoghurt becomes. (This recipe makes about 600 ml – any leftover yoghurt can be stored in the fridge for up to 2 weeks.)

To make the dressing, combine all the ingredients, along with 3 tablespoons of the coconut yoghurt, in a small bowl.

Heat the oil or fat in a large frying pan over medium heat. Add the garlic and cook for 20 seconds until softened and fragrant. Toss in the kale and sauté for 1 minute, then add 3 tablespoons of water and continue to cook, stirring occasionally, for about 3–4 minutes, or until the kale is slightly wilted and cooked through. Add the pine nuts and chilli flakes (if using), season with salt and pepper and remove from the heat.

Place the sautéed kale on a platter, drizzle over the dressing and scatter some extra pine nuts over the top. Serve.

SERVES 4

TIP

Leftover coconut yoghurt will keep in the fridge for up to 2 weeks. Add it to smoothies, dressings or the top of some paleo muesli (see recipe, page 101).

Raw cauliflower tabouli

I've replaced the burghul (cracked wheat) in tabouli with cauliflower, which means that you still get the satisfying texture without any of the problems that go along with eating wheat. I also like to add toasted sesame seeds or activated nuts for extra crunch – try almonds, walnuts or macadamias. Chopped avocado is another great addition, as are smoked fish, grilled prawns or leftover roast chicken or lamb. Pretty much anything goes! You can eat this on its own for lunch, or serve it alongside some paprika chicken (see recipe, page 165) or stuffed mushrooms (see recipe, page 168).

½ head of cauliflower (about 500 g), cut into florets

4 tablespoons chopped flat-leaf parsley leaves

2 tablespoons chopped mint leaves

1 large fennel bulb, finely diced

1 red onion, finely diced

2 Lebanese cucumbers, chopped

8 fresh okra pods*, sliced into thin rounds

1 carrot, cut into batons

2 tomatoes, cut into large cubes

sea salt and freshly ground black pepper

1 tablespoon sesame seeds, toasted

Dressing

125 ml (½ cup) lemon juice

4 tablespoons extra-virgin olive oil

1 garlic clove, crushed

2 teaspoons ground sumac*, plus extra to serve

1 teaspoon ground cumin

** See Setting Up Your Paleo Kitchen*

Place the cauliflower in a food processor and process until it resembles coarse rice grains. Transfer to a large serving bowl.

To make the dressing, whisk all the ingredients together and set aside.

Combine the parsley, mint, fennel, onion, cucumber, okra, carrot and tomato with the cauliflower. Pour on the dressing and mix until well combined. Season with salt and pepper, then leave to marinate for 10 minutes.

To serve, sprinkle with the toasted sesame seeds and a little extra sumac. Serve immediately.

SERVES 4–6

Raw rainbow pad Thai

If there is one dish in this book that I urge you to try, it has to be this one. This salad has everything – colour, texture, aroma, simplicity and, of course, flavour. It's really important to include some vegetables as part of every meal. Of course, gorgeous salads like this are a great way of doing this, but if I am really short of time, I just grab a whole carrot, cucumber or even fennel bulb and stick it on my plate with a drizzle of raw apple cider vinegar or sauerkraut juice to accompany my main meal and off we go.

- 1 large carrot
- 1 large zucchini
- 1 red capsicum, deseeded, finely sliced into long thin strips
- ⅛ red cabbage, finely shredded
- 2 long red chillies, deseeded and finely sliced lengthways
- 2 spring onions, cut into 5-cm batons and finely sliced lengthways
- 50 g (⅓ cup) cashew or macadamia nuts (activated if possible, see page 198), chopped
- sesame seeds, toasted, to serve
- coriander leaves, to serve
- 1 lime, cut into quarters, to serve

Dressing

- 3 tablespoons almond butter
- 3 tablespoons lime juice
- 2½ tablespoons tamari or coconut aminos*
- 1 teaspoon fish sauce
- 3 teaspoons honey (optional)
- 1 teaspoon sesame oil
- 1½ teaspoons finely grated ginger
- 1 garlic clove, crushed

* *See Setting Up Your Paleo Kitchen*

To make the dressing, place all the ingredients and 3 tablespoons of water in a bowl and mix until combined. Set aside until needed.

Use a vegetable peeler to shave the carrot and zucchini lengthways (or you can finely slice with a sharp knife). Cut each slice lengthways again into thin, noodle-like strips.

Place the carrot, zucchini, capsicum, cabbage, chilli and spring onion in a large bowl, pour on the dressing and gently toss through with your hands to combine. Allow to stand for 10–15 minutes before serving so that the veggies absorb the lovely dressing.

Transfer the pad Thai to serving bowls, sprinkle with the nuts, sesame seeds and coriander leaves and serve with the lime wedges on the side.

SERVES 2

Tomato and pomegranate chopped salad

Summer is the time for tomatoes and fresh vibrant salads like this one. It's so simple to make and is perfect teamed with a piece of grilled steak, good-quality snags, barbecued tuna or roast lamb.

- 3 tomatoes, deseeded and cut into 5-mm dice
- 150 g yellow cherry tomatoes, cut into 5-mm dice
- 150 g cherry tomatoes, cut into 5-mm dice
- 1 red capsicum, deseeded and cut into 5-mm dice
- ½ red onion, finely diced
- seeds of 1 small pomegranate
- 1 tablespoon chopped mint leaves, plus extra to garnish

Dressing

- 2 garlic cloves, crushed
- ½ teaspoon ground allspice
- ¼ teaspoon ground cumin
- 3 teaspoons apple cider vinegar or lemon juice
- 1½ tablespoons pomegranate molasses (see note) or coconut aminos*
- 3 tablespoons extra-virgin olive oil, plus extra to serve
- sea salt and freshly ground black pepper

* *See Setting Up Your Paleo Kitchen*

Note

Pomegranate molasses is a thick, glossy reduction of pomegranate juice with a sweet and sour flavour. It's available from most supermarkets and Middle Eastern grocers.

Combine all the salad ingredients in a large bowl and set aside.

To make the dressing, whisk all the ingredients together in a small bowl.

Pour the dressing over the tomato and pomegranate salad and mix gently to combine.

Spoon the salad onto a large platter, garnish with a sprinkle of mint and drizzle over some extra olive oil to finish.

SERVES 4

Asian mushroom salad

Mushrooms were my worst enemy as a kid – I hated them, and mum would sneak them into all types of meals. Luckily I was onto her tricks and caught her out more times than I can remember. Fast forward ten years and I had fallen in love with mushrooms and couldn't get enough of them! If you are a mushroom fan then give this salad a go. It works well with poached chook or a lovely braised short rib.

- 4 duck eggs (or regular eggs)
- 2 tablespoons coconut oil
- 100 g wood ear fungus (see note), torn into pieces
- 100 g shimeji mushrooms
- 150 g oyster mushrooms, sliced
- 150 g shiitake mushrooms, sliced
- sea salt and freshly ground black pepper
- 2 large handfuls of water spinach (see note) or other greens
- 100 g enoki mushrooms, separated
- 80 g water chestnuts, thinly sliced
- 3 tablespoons finely sliced garlic, fried until crispy
- 1 tablespoon black and white sesame seeds, toasted

Dressing

- 4 tablespoons macadamia oil or extra-virgin olive oil
- 1 tablespoon grated ginger
- 3 tablespoons tamari or coconut aminos*
- 1 teaspoon grated lemon zest
- ½ teaspoon dried chilli flakes

** See Setting Up Your Paleo Kitchen*

Note

Brown and ear-shaped, wood ear fungus are commonly used in Chinese cuisine. Water spinach is also known as morning glory and is popular in South-East Asia. Both are available from Asian grocers.

Fill a saucepan with water and bring to the boil over high heat. Turn down to a simmer, carefully add the eggs and simmer for 7 minutes, or until the eggs are cooked to your liking. Drain and place the eggs in cold water and, when cool enough to handle, peel. Cut the eggs in half and set aside until needed.

To make the dressing, combine all the ingredients in a bowl and mix well.

Heat a wok or large frying pan over medium–high heat. Add the oil and sauté the wood ear fungus and the shimeji, oyster and shiitake mushrooms in batches for 2–3 minutes, or until tender. Season with salt and pepper. Place the mushroom mixture in a large bowl, then mix in the water spinach, enoki mushrooms, water chestnuts, crispy garlic and dressing.

Arrange the salad on a platter, top with the eggs and sprinkle with the sesame seeds.

SERVES 4

Moroccan carrot salad

You can have this salad on the table in less than 10 minutes and it has probably received the biggest response out of all the salads in this book when I've made it for friends. The secret is in the dressing, which includes ginger and sumac. If you're trying to avoid as much sugar as you can, just omit the dried barberries or currants.

- 4 tablespoons extra-virgin olive oil
- 1 tablespoon lemon juice
- 1 tablespoon apple cider vinegar
- 1 teaspoon grated ginger
- 1 long red chilli, deseeded and finely chopped (optional)
- ½ teaspoon ground sumac*
- 4 large carrots, grated
- 1 handful of almonds (activated if possible, see page 198), toasted and chopped
- 1 large handful of chopped coriander leaves
- 1 handful of chopped mint leaves
- 3 tablespoons dried barberries (see note) or currants
- sea salt and freshly ground black pepper

** See Setting Up Your Paleo Kitchen*

Note

Barberries are Iranian berries with a sweet and sour flavour. They can be found at health food stores and specialty food stores.

In a large serving bowl, whisk together the olive oil, lemon juice, vinegar and ginger until well combined. Add the chilli (if using), sumac, carrot, almonds, coriander, mint and barberries or currants.

Toss, season with salt and pepper and serve alongside your favourite protein or as part of a spread of salads at a barbecue.

SERVES 4–6

Sautéed silverbeet with garlic and hazelnuts

In the past I have talked about wanting to bring meatloaf back into fashion – and I think we have just about managed to do it! But now I'd like to do the same for silverbeet, which is one of the most underrated vegetables on the planet. It really is a superfood, not only for our health but also because it is so sustainable and very easy to grow in the smallest of spaces. This is a great side dish that goes with almost everything and can be made in a matter of minutes. You could also add some free-range bacon or lamb mince to this dish to make it a simple but satisfying main.

- 1 bunch of silverbeet (about 300 g)
- 3 tablespoons coconut oil
- 3 garlic cloves, sliced
- 3 tablespoons hazelnuts, roasted, skins removed and roughly chopped, plus extra to serve
- 1 large handful of baby beetroot leaves or sorrel leaves
- sea salt and freshly ground black pepper
- extra-virgin olive oil, to serve
- lemon halves, to serve

Remove the central stalks from the silverbeet, reserving the leaves and a single stalk (the remaining stalks can be saved for a soup or broth). Chop the stalk and set aside with the leaves.

Heat the oil in a large frying pan over medium heat. Add the garlic and cook for 20 seconds, until softened and fragrant. Add the chopped silverbeet stalk and sauté for 1 minute. Add the leaves and 3 tablespoons of water and continue to cook for 3 minutes, stirring occasionally, until the silverbeet is slightly wilted. Toss through the hazelnuts and beetroot or sorrel leaves and season with sea salt and pepper.

To serve, place the sautéed silverbeet on a platter, drizzle with a little extra-virgin olive oil, squeeze over some lemon juice and scatter more hazelnuts nuts over the top.

SERVES 4

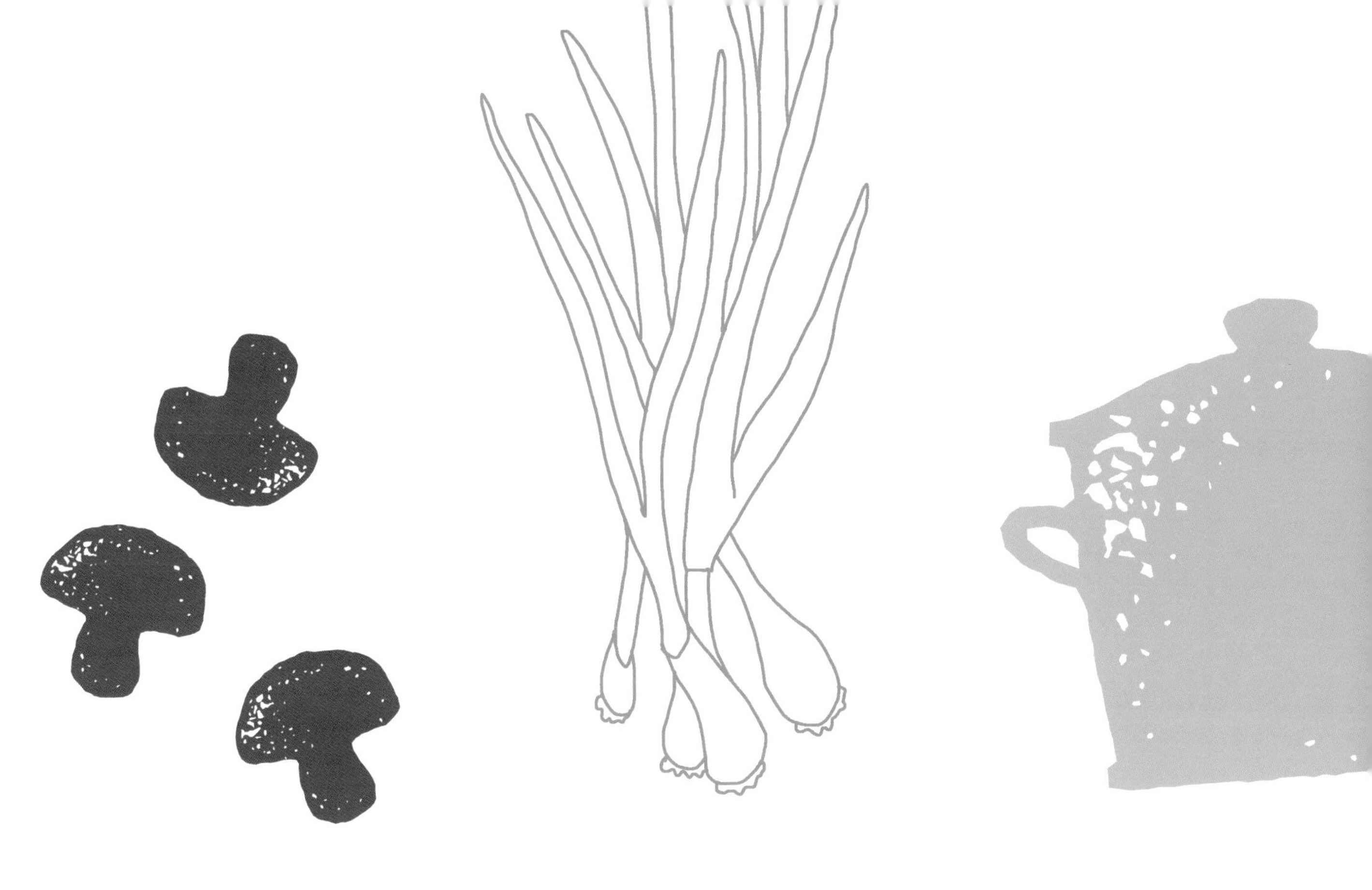

MAIN MEALS

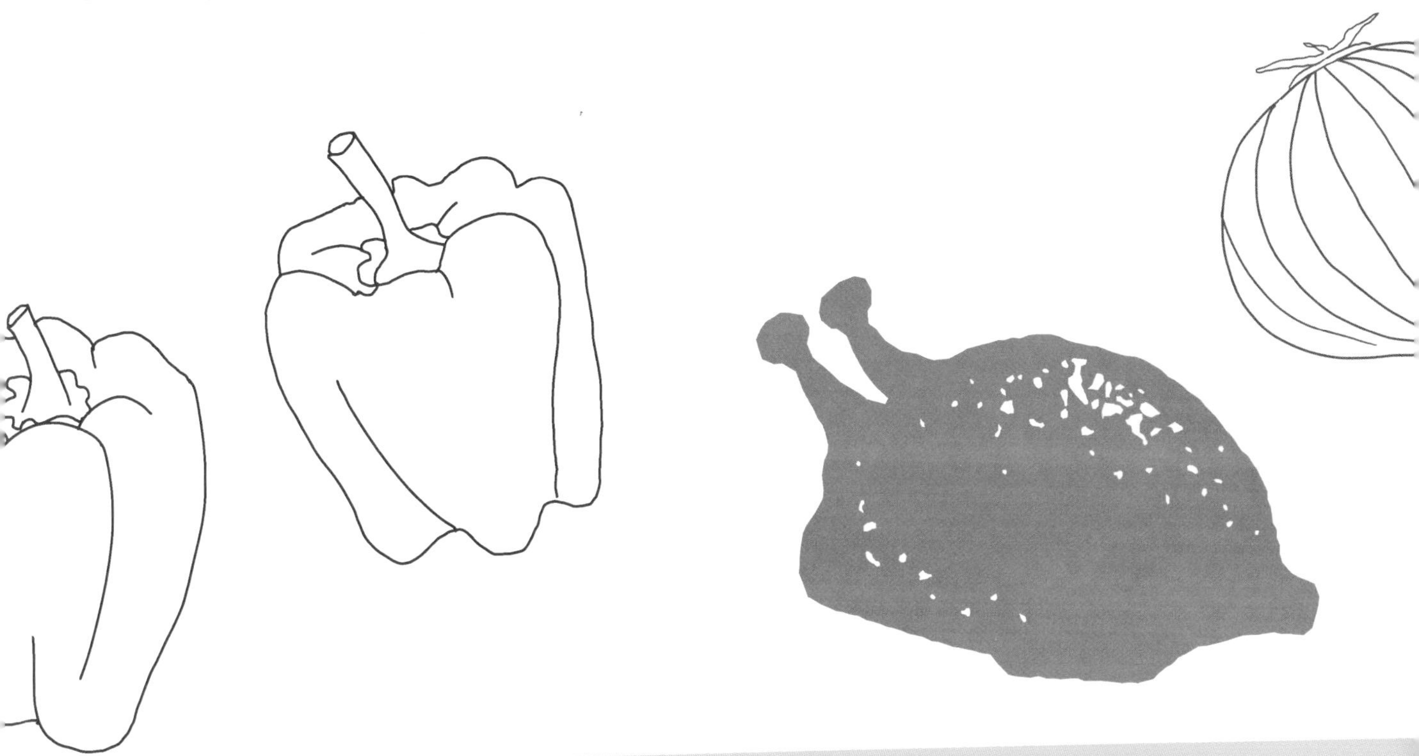

Lemongrass prawn skewers

I get so many of my paleo ideas from South East Asian cookery as they are absolute masters of flavour. As well as being delicious, this dish is also heaps of fun as everyone around the table gets to make their own little prawn rolls. You will definitely want to have these for lunch the next day so, as always, make sure you double the recipe! Serve with some kimchi (see recipe, page 110) on the side.

- 600 g raw king prawns, shelled, deveined and diced
- 1 tablespoon fish sauce
- 1 garlic clove, finely chopped
- 1 long red chilli, deseeded and finely chopped
- 1 spring onion, finely sliced
- 1 tablespoon iced water
- 5 tablespoons sesame seeds
- 3 long thin lemongrass stalks, cut into 8-cm sticks (you'll need 12 sticks in total)
- 80 ml (⅓ cup) coconut oil, melted
- sea salt and freshly ground black pepper
- 1 lime, halved
- 1 Lebanese cucumber, halved lengthways and sliced
- 1 carrot, julienned
- 150 g bean sprouts
- Vietnamese mint, Thai basil and coriander leaves, to serve
- baby cos lettuce leaves, to serve

Lime dipping sauce

- 1 small red chilli, roughly chopped
- 1 garlic clove, chopped
- 2 tablespoons fish sauce
- juice of 2 limes
- 3 tablespoons water

To make the lime dipping sauce, pound the chilli and garlic using a mortar and pestle until almost smooth. Stir in the remaining ingredients. Taste and add more fish sauce or lime juice if necessary. Set aside.

Process the prawns in a food processor until smooth and sticky. Add the fish sauce, garlic, chilli and spring onion and pulse to combine. Add the water and pulse to form a thick, coarse paste.

Brush your hands with oil or water, then divide the prawn mixture into 12 equal portions. Roll them into sausage shapes.

Place the sesame seeds in a small bowl and roll the prawn sausages in the seeds to coat. Thread the prawn sausages onto the lemongrass sticks and roll them in the sesame seeds again. Brush with a little oil.

Preheat a barbecue or large frying pan to hot and brush with the coconut oil. Cook the prawn skewers for 5 minutes, turning occasionally, until golden and cooked through. Sprinkle with a little salt and pepper, then squeeze over some lime juice.

Place the prawn skewers, cucumber, carrot, sprouts, herbs and lettuce leaves on serving plates and the dipping sauce in a small bowl. Allow your guests to fill their own lettuce leaf with the prawn skewers, vegetables, herbs and dipping sauce. Make sure you remove the lemongrass sticks from the prawn skewers before eating them!

SERVES 4

Chorizo and seafood 'paella'

What could be more tantalising than the smell of smoked paprika, garlic and seafood roasting in the pan? Not much in my book, and that is why I adore this recipe. This paleo 'paella' has the flavour of a traditional Spanish paella, but is far more nutritious as it uses cauliflower instead of rice. By using cauliflower, you also cut down on your cooking time, which is definitely something to celebrate!

- 500 ml (2 cups) Chicken Bone Broth (see recipe, page 256)
- 2 pinches of saffron threads
- 1 head of cauliflower, coarsely chopped
- 2 tablespoons coconut oil or other good-quality fat*
- 150 g chorizo sausage, thickly sliced
- 1 red capsicum, deseeded and diced
- 2 tomatoes, diced
- 1 large onion, finely chopped
- 4 garlic cloves, crushed
- 1 tablespoon tomato paste
- 1 teaspoon sweet paprika
- 1 tablespoon smoked paprika, plus extra to serve
- 1 small handful of flat-leaf parsley, leaves and stalks chopped separately
- 8 raw king prawns, shelled and deveined with tails intact
- 400 g mussels, cleaned
- 300 g clams, cleaned
- sea salt and freshly ground black pepper
- extra-virgin olive oil, to drizzle
- juice of ½ lemon

* *See Setting Up Your Paleo Kitchen*

Pour the bone broth into a saucepan, place over medium heat and bring to a simmer. Remove from the heat, stir in the saffron threads and set aside to infuse for 5–10 minutes.

Meanwhile, put the cauliflower into the bowl of a food processor and process into tiny pieces resembling grains of rice. Set aside.

Heat the oil or fat in a large, deep frying pan over medium heat, add the chorizo and fry, turning once, until golden and crispy, about 1 minute. Stir in the capsicum, tomato, onion, garlic, tomato paste and sweet and smoked paprika and cook until the vegetables have softened, 2–3 minutes. Pour in the warm bone broth, add the parsley stalks and bring to the boil. Add the prawns, mussels and clams, cover with a lid and cook for 2–3 minutes, until the mussels and clams have opened and the prawns are cooked. Stir through the cauliflower, cook for 2 minutes, then season with salt and pepper.

To serve, transfer the paella to a large serving bowl. Garnish with the parsley leaves, drizzle with the olive oil and lemon juice, and sprinkle with a little extra smoked paprika.

SERVES 4

Barbecued wild fish with smoky chorizo salad

Whenever I think about fast food, my first thought is always seafood as it is extremely easy and quick to cook. This dish is a delicious and healthy dinner when you don't have much time. Just make sure you look for chorizo made with free-range pork, and don't forget a salad and some fermented vegetables on the side!

- 4 × 180 g wild fish fillets (such as mackerel, snapper, flathead or bream), skin left on
- sea salt and freshly ground black pepper
- 2 tablespoons coconut oil or other good-quality fat*, melted
- baby basil leaves, to garnish

Smoky chorizo salad

- 450 g chorizo sausage, cut in half lengthways
- 12 cherry tomatoes, quartered
- 1 handful of chopped flat-leaf parsley leaves
- 2 garlic cloves, crushed
- 4 tablespoons extra-virgin olive oil
- 1 tablespoon finely grated lemon zest
- 2 tablespoons lemon juice
- 1 teaspoon cumin seeds, lightly toasted
- sea salt and freshly ground black pepper

** See Setting Up Your Paleo Kitchen*

Heat your barbecue to medium–high.

To make the salad, cook the chorizo on the barbecue until browned and cooked through, about 1–2 minutes on each side. Remove from the barbecue, finely dice and place in a bowl. Add the tomato, parsley, garlic, olive oil, lemon zest, lemon juice and cumin seeds and toss to combine. Season with salt and pepper.

To prepare the fish, season the fillets with salt and pepper and rub both sides with the coconut oil or fat. Put the fillets skin-side up on the barbecue, cover them with foil and cook until golden brown, about 3 minutes. Remove the foil, flip the fillets with a spatula and cook the fish until they are completely opaque throughout and the skin is golden and crisp, about 5 minutes more. Place the fish on a serving plate and serve topped with the salad and garnished with the baby basil.

SERVES 4

Sashimi salad

Just looking at this dish makes me so happy to be alive and eating this way. I love using tuna, ocean trout, Atlantic salmon and kingfish, but you could also try grilled prawns, whiting fillets or barbecued squid.

- 1 Lebanese cucumber, halved lengthways and deseeded
- 1 large carrot
- ¼ daikon*
- ½ kohlrabi (see note)
- 500 g sashimi-grade fish, very finely sliced
- 1 large handful of mizuna leaves (see note)
- 1 avocado, sliced
- ½ red onion, finely sliced
- 2 long green chillies, deseeded and finely sliced (optional)

Dressing

- 4 tablespoons tamari
- 2½ tablespoons lime juice or apple cider vinegar
- pinch of freshly ground black pepper
- 1 teaspoon finely grated ginger
- 3 tablespoons dried bonito flakes (see note)
- 2 teaspoons macadamia oil
- 2 teaspoons sesame oil

To serve

- wasabi
- black and white sesame seeds, toasted
- tobiko (see note)
- pickled ginger

** See Setting Up Your Paleo Kitchen*

To make the dressing, combine the tamari, 1 tablespoon of water, the lime juice or vinegar, pepper, ginger and bonito flakes in a bowl, then mix well. Allow to stand for 1 hour. Strain the tamari mixture into another bowl, pressing all the liquid through and discarding the bonito flakes. Add the macadamia oil and sesame oil to the tamari mixture and mix well.

Finely slice the cucumber, carrot, daikon and kohlrabi lengthways using a mandoline or sharp knife, then cut into thin strips.

Arrange your fish and each of the salad ingredients on a platter. Pour the dressing into a small serving bowl and place on the platter. Serve the sashimi salad with the wasabi, sesame seeds, tobiko and pickled ginger on the side.

SERVES 4

Note

Kohlrabi is a bulbous, alien-like vegetable that is related to cabbage and can be eaten raw or cooked. Its flavour is similar to broccoli stem and it's available from some greengrocers and supermarkets. Mizuna is a Japanese herb with a mild, peppery flavour; bonito flakes are made from fermented bonito fish; and tobiko is flying fish roe. All can be found at Asian grocers.

Herb and garlic fish parcels

Stick a piece of fish in a bag with some herbs, cherry tomatoes and a little garlic, then wrap it up and bake until tender. This recipe really is that simple. You can even make these parcels up to a day before (no more) and then just pop them in the oven when your guests arrive. I like to serve them with a big platter of sautéed greens (see recipe, page 122) and some fermented veg on the side (see recipe, page 116).

- 2 × 180 g snapper fillets
- sea salt and freshly ground black pepper
- 10 clams, cleaned
- 4 garlic cloves, crushed
- 100 ml coconut oil or other good-quality fat*, melted
- 4 tablespoons chopped flat-leaf parsley leaves
- 1 long red chilli, deseeded and finely chopped
- 4 tablespoons dry white wine (such as chardonnay)
- 10 cherry tomatoes
- zest and juice of 1 lemon
- 1 teaspoon grated bottarga (see note)

** See Setting Up Your Paleo Kitchen*

Note

Bottarga is the dried pressed roe of mullet or tuna and is available at specialty food stores. Alternatively, add 1 chopped anchovy fillet to the mixture you spoon over the fish.

Preheat the oven to 200°C. Place two large sheets of baking paper (each piece should be large enough to enclose a fish fillet and half of the clams) side by side in a large roasting tin.

Season the fish with salt and pepper and place a fillet in the centre of each piece of baking paper.

In a bowl, mix together the clams, garlic, oil or fat, parsley, chilli, wine, tomatoes and lemon zest and juice, then spoon over the fish, dividing the mixture evenly. Fold each piece of paper over from two sides to form a package, then fold in the ends to seal. Bake in the oven until the fish is cooked through and the clams are open, about 10–12 minutes.

To serve, place each packet on a serving plate, open and sprinkle with the bottarga.

SERVES 2

Chilled avocado soup with poached prawns and mango

I would love to write a book that has 101 ways with avocados, as they are a favourite of mine. They are full of beneficial mono-unsaturated fats and their creamy texture lends itself to so many different recipes. This soup is perfect for when avocados are in season and inexpensive. If you have heaps of avocados to get through, you can make a double batch of this and freeze it for later. I have teamed it with prawns but it also works well with crab, mussels, lobster, scampi, scallops, sea urchin or even roasted or poached chicken. Pop some sauerkraut (see recipe, page 121) or kimchi (see recipe, page 110) on top too if you like.

- 8 raw king prawns
- 600 ml Chicken Bone Broth (see recipe, page 256)
- 500 ml (2 cups) coconut milk
- 1 green chilli, deseeded and chopped, plus extra to serve (optional)
- 1 teaspoon grated ginger
- ½ teaspoon ground cumin
- 2 avocados, peeled and pitted
- ½ cup chopped coriander leaves, plus extra to serve
- 4 teaspoons lime juice
- sea salt and freshly ground black pepper
- ½ ripe mango, peeled, pitted and diced
- 1 teaspoon olive oil

Cook the prawns in salted boiling water until pink and firm, about 2–3 minutes. Transfer to a bowl of ice-cold water and leave until the prawns are completely cold. Peel, devein and cut the prawns into 1-cm pieces.

Place the chicken broth, coconut milk, chilli, ginger and cumin in a large saucepan and bring to the boil over medium heat. Reduce the heat to medium–low and simmer for 5 minutes. Remove from the heat and leave to cool.

Once cool, pour the chicken and coconut broth into a blender, add the avocado, coriander and 3 teaspoons of the lime juice and blend until smooth and creamy (add more stock or water to thin if necessary). Season with salt and pepper to taste. Place in the fridge to chill (or serve at room temperature if desired).

Put the mango, oil, extra chilli (if using), chopped prawns and remaining lime juice in a small bowl and toss well. Season with a pinch of salt.

Ladle the avocado soup into serving bowls. Evenly divide the mango and prawn salad between the bowls and finish with some coriander leaves.

SERVES 4

Sichuan chicken salad with egg 'noodles'

This Asian-inspired salad with egg 'noodles' will be a hit with the kids and won't leave you with the usual heavy feeling you get after eating wheat-based noodles.

- 600 g boneless chicken thigh fillets, skin on
- 2 tablespoons coconut oil, melted
- sea salt and freshly ground black pepper
- 1 Lebanese cucumber
- 2 spring onions, cut into batons
- 1 handful of coriander leaves
- 2 long red chillies, deseeded and sliced into batons
- 50 g enoki mushrooms
- 100 g Chinese cabbage, shredded
- 40 g bean sprouts
- toasted sesame seeds, to serve

Egg 'noodles'

- 8 eggs
- freshly ground black pepper
- 1½ teaspoons fish sauce
- 1 teaspoon tamari
- 1 tablespoon coconut oil

Dressing

- 1 teaspoon finely grated ginger
- 1 garlic clove, crushed
- 2½ tablespoons tamari
- 1½ tablespoons sesame oil
- 2 tablespoons apple cider vinegar
- 2 tablespoons macadamia oil or extra-virgin olive oil
- 1 teaspoon coarsely ground Sichuan pepper, toasted, plus extra to serve

To make the eggs 'noodles', place the eggs, a little pepper, fish sauce and tamari in a large bowl and mix well with a fork to combine. Melt 1 teaspoon of the oil in a wok or large frying pan over medium–high heat. Pour about one-quarter of the egg mixture into the pan, swirl to form a thin layer and cook for 30 seconds. Flip and cook for another minute on the other side, then transfer the omelette to a chopping board. Repeat this process until you have used all the egg mixture. Thinly slice the omelettes into strips and set aside.

To make the dressing, combine all of the ingredients in a bowl with 2 tablespoons of water.

Coat the chicken in 2 teaspoons of the melted oil and season with salt and pepper.

Heat the remaining oil in a frying pan over medium–high heat, add the chicken and cook for 5 minutes on each side, or until completely cooked through. Set aside and keep warm.

Cut the cucumber lengthways, scoop out and discard the seeds. Slice the cucumber into thin strips.

Place the cucumber, spring onion, coriander leaves, chilli, enoki mushrooms, cabbage and bean sprouts in a bowl and toss well. Add half of the dressing and toss again to combine.

Arrange the noodles on four serving plates and top with the salad and chicken. Spoon some more dressing over the chicken and sprinkle with the sesame seeds and extra Sichuan pepper.

SERVES 4

Helen's creamy chicken and cabbage salad

We always have some type of protein cooked and ready to go in the fridge at home. It takes a little bit of planning, but once you are in the swing of it, it's super easy. My advice is to cook up a couple of chickens during the week – you could roast the chooks, strip the meat off and make a broth from the bones, or you could poach them in a stock before stripping the meat off. In both cases you are left with a nutritious broth to drink on its own or add to soups, braises or curries, as well as the chicken meat, which you can use to whip up a healthy meal. Having this protein ready to go in the fridge at all times is going to stop you eating less desirable foods. This recipe comes from my good friend, naturopath Helen Padarin, and it's one of my favourite ways to use the chicken in our fridge. You've got quality protein mixed with good fats and fibrous veggies, and you can have it on the table in less than 15 minutes. You can't argue with that!

- 1 avocado, diced
- 500 g savoy cabbage, shredded
- 200 g leftover roast chicken, shredded
- 3 tablespoons extra-virgin olive oil
- 3 tablespoons lemon juice
- sea salt and freshly ground black pepper
- 2 tablespoons pine nuts, toasted

Mash the avocado slightly to a creamy and slightly chunky texture in a bowl, then add the cabbage, roast chicken, olive oil and lemon juice and give everything a good toss so the avocado dresses the salad nicely. Season with salt and pepper.

Arrange the salad on a platter and sprinkle the pine nuts over the top. Serve.

SERVES 2

TIP

Leftover poached chicken will also work beautifully in this salad – see recipe on page 156.

Chicken cacciatore

Chicken cacciatore is a classic Italian dish with a rich tomato and herb sauce. Get the best quality chicken legs you can find and make sure you double the quantity, as it is even tastier for lunch the next day. I often add chicken livers to this dish, as they are high is protein, iron, folate and vitamin A – and they taste fabulous. If you'd like to give them a go, simply fry some chicken livers in a little coconut oil in a separate pan until they are pink, then fold them into the sauce at the end.

- 3 tablespoons coconut oil or other good-quality fat*
- 1 onion, chopped
- 3 garlic cloves, crushed
- 1 × 1.8 kg chicken, cut into 8 pieces
- 200 ml dry white wine (such as chardonnay)
- 2 × 400 g cans whole peeled tomatoes
- 1 bay leaf
- 1 teaspoon finely chopped rosemary leaves
- ½ cup black olives, pitted (optional)
- 3 tablespoons chopped flat-leaf parsley leaves, plus extra to serve
- sea salt and freshly ground black pepper
- 250 ml (1 cup) Chicken Bone Broth (see recipe, page 256)
- 1½ tablespoons apple cider vinegar

Zucchini 'noodles'

- 2 zucchini
- 1 tablespoon coconut oil
- 1 garlic clove, crushed
- sea salt and freshly ground black pepper

** See Setting Up Your Paleo Kitchen*

Preheat the oven to 160°C.

Heat the oil in a large casserole dish or large, deep, ovenproof frying pan over medium heat. Add the onion and cook for 8 minutes until translucent. Stir in the garlic and cook for a further 30–60 seconds. Push the onion and garlic to the side of the pan, add the chicken pieces and cook for 3 minutes on each side, or until golden.

Add the wine and cook until almost evaporated (5 minutes). Add the tomatoes, bay leaf, rosemary, olives (if using) and parsley and season with salt and pepper. Cover and place in the oven to cook for about 1 hour, gradually adding the bone broth as the pan juices evaporate and turning the chicken pieces a few times to make sure they cook evenly.

While the chicken is cooking, make the zucchini 'noodles'. Cut the zucchini into very thin strips using a mandoline, vegetable peeler or sharp knife. You could also create spaghetti-like strips by using a vegetable spiraliser. Heat the coconut oil in a frying pan over medium–high heat, add the zucchini and garlic and sauté for a few minutes until slightly soft. Season with salt and pepper. Keep warm until ready to serve.

Once the chicken is cooked through (the juices will run clear when chicken is pierced with a skewer), remove from the oven and stir through the apple cider vinegar. Scatter over the extra parsley and serve with the zucchini noodles on the side.

SERVES 4–6

Healing chicken and vegetable soup

People around the world have known about the healing benefits of chicken soup for millennia. It is as powerful a medicine as ever – helping to heal the lining of your gut, boosting immunity and contributing to the health of your joints. Just remember that it's essential to use homemade chicken bone broth in this recipe to get maximum nutritional benefit.

1 × 1.6 kg chicken
Chicken Bone Broth (see recipe, page 256)
2 tablespoons coconut oil or other good-quality fat *
1 onion, chopped
3 garlic cloves, crushed
1 large carrot, chopped
1 celery stalk, halved lengthways and cut into 1-cm thick slices
4 thyme sprigs
1 bay leaf
1 tablespoon finely grated ginger
1 large zucchini, halved lengthways and sliced into 2-cm thick slices
300 g kent or butternut pumpkin, peeled and cut into 2-cm cubes
200 g silverbeet, shredded
sea salt and freshly ground black pepper
1 handful of flat-leaf parsley leaves, finely chopped (optional)

** See Setting Up Your Paleo Kitchen*

First, we're going to poach the whole chicken in the bone broth. To do this, follow the chicken bone broth recipe on page 256. After you have simmered the stock for 24 hours (and before adding the parsley) remove some of the bones from the broth and add the whole chicken. The chicken needs to be completely submerged, so add more water if necessary. Simmer, uncovered, for 1 hour, or until the chicken is cooked through. About 10 minutes before the chicken is ready, add the parsley. Carefully remove the chicken from the broth and allow to cool slightly. When cool enough to handle, shred the flesh and discard the bones. Cover and refrigerate until needed.

To finish making your broth, continue to follow the instructions for straining and skimming on page 256.

Place a stockpot or very large saucepan over medium heat and coat the base with the oil or fat. Add the onion, garlic, carrot, celery, thyme and bay leaf and cook, stirring, for about 6 minutes until the vegetables are softened but not browned. Pour in 1.75 litres of the chicken bone broth and bring to the boil, then turn down to a simmer and cook for 20 minutes.

Add the ginger, zucchini and pumpkin to the pan and continue to cook for a further 15 minutes, or until the vegetables are tender. Add 400–500 g of the shredded poached chicken and the silverbeet and continue to simmer for another few minutes until the silverbeet is cooked and the chicken is warmed through. Season, sprinkle with the parsley (if using) and serve.

SERVES 6

TIP

Poaching a whole chicken in bone broth, as I do in this recipe, adds so much extra flavour and goodness. Leftover shredded chicken can be used in cauliflower fried rice (see recipe, page 166), salads (see recipes, pages 160 and 153) or little celery boats (see recipe, page 209).

Vietnamese chicken wings

When I was a kid, I loved it when my mum made chicken wings – I always enjoyed sitting at the table and nibbling the meat around the bones. From my experience, most kids love finger foods, so this is a great dish to try making for them. Simply reduce or even omit the chilli, depending on what your kids are used to. And if you don't want to miss out on the chilli kick, simply have some kimchi or paleo sriracha chilli sauce on the side for yourself (see recipes, pages 110 and 249). You could also use chicken drumsticks or marylands for this if you wanted something a little less fiddly. Serve with a big cucumber salad or some sautéed Asian greens. And if you have any wings left over, why not remove the meat and add it to some cauliflower fried rice (see recipe, page 166), pop it in a chicken bone broth (see recipe, page 256) with some greens, or just add it to some scrambled eggs for brekkie.

- 2 tablespoons tamari or coconut aminos*
- 2 tablespoons coconut oil or other good-quality fat*, melted
- 1 tablespoon fish sauce
- 1 teaspoon honey (optional)
- 4 garlic cloves, crushed
- 2 spring onions, finely chopped
- 1 teaspoon dried chilli flakes
- ½ teaspoon Chinese five spice
- 12 chicken wings
- 1 small handful of mixed Thai basil leaves, coriander leaves and Vietnamese mint leaves

Fried shallots and chillies

- 250 ml (1 cup) coconut oil
- 4 French shallots, finely sliced
- 2 long red chillies, thinly sliced

** See Setting Up Your Paleo Kitchen*

To make the marinade, combine the tamari or coconut aminos, oil or fat, fish sauce, honey (if using), garlic, spring onion, chilli flakes and Chinese five spice in a large bowl and whisk well.

Add the chicken wings to the marinade and turn until the chicken is well coated. Cover and refrigerate for at least 1 hour, or ideally overnight.

Preheat the oven to 200°C.

Transfer the wings to a baking tray, spread out in an even layer, then roast, turning occasionally, for 25–30 minutes until the chicken is golden and cooked through.

Meanwhile, to make the fried shallots, melt the oil or fat in a small saucepan over medium heat. Add the shallots and cook for 2–3 minutes until golden. Remove the shallots with a slotted spoon and drain on paper towel.

To make the fried chillies, add the sliced chilli to the same coconut oil and cook for a few minutes, or until the chilli starts to turn a light golden. Remove with a slotted spoon and drain on paper towel. (The coconut oil will have taken on a lovely flavour from the shallots and chilli. You can re-use it for sautéing vegetables or cooking meat, chicken or fish.)

Arrange the chicken wings on a serving platter and sprinkle with the Asian herbs and as many fried shallots and chillies as desired. Any leftover fried shallots or chillies can be stored in an airtight container for up to 1 week.

SERVES 4

Chopped chicken salad with bacon and sherry vinaigrette

This simple chicken salad is a celebration of fresh and vibrant ingredients. It's full of good fats from the nuts, avocado and egg, and you can increase the fat content further by serving the salad with delicious homemade mayonnaise (see recipe, page 250). Our brains are 70% fat, so these kinds of good fats have been a fundamental dietary staple since Palaeolithic times and contribute to healthy brain functioning.

- 1 dill frond, leaves picked
- 1 sprig of parsley, leaves picked
- 1 small handful of chives, snipped into 5-cm lengths
- 1 sprig of chervil, leaves picked
- 60 g pine nuts, lightly toasted
- ½ avocado, sliced
- 2 Hard-boiled Eggs (see recipe, page 197), cut in half
- 300 g leftover roast or poached chicken, shredded
- 1 cucumber, halved, seeds removed and julienned
- 1 celery stalk, julienned
- 1 carrot, julienned
- 1 handful of watercress leaves
- 5 brussels sprouts, finely shredded
- Bacon and Sherry Vinaigrette (see recipe, page 241)
- Sauerkraut with Dill and Juniper Berries (see recipe, page 121)

Combine the dill, parsley, chives and chervil in a small bowl.

Arrange the pine nuts in a straight line on a serving board or platter. Place the avocado slices next to the nuts, followed by a row of the mixed herbs. Follow with the hard-boiled eggs, shredded chicken, cucumber, celery, carrot, watercress and brussels sprouts.

Drizzle the dressing over the salad and serve with a jar of sauerkraut.

SERVES 2

Chicken liver curry

I know this recipe might not be everyone's cup of tea, but I love it and it's just bursting with nutrition and goodness. If you are not keen on livers, how about starting off by replacing them with chicken thighs (which will need to be cooked a little longer) and then add two or three livers into the dish. This would mean about 10 percent of the dish is livers – you could gradually work your way up to eating more or just keep it like this. Even having a few livers in the dish makes it more beneficial to your health. There are no veggies in this curry, so perhaps serve it with some broccoli or cauliflower rice (see recipe, page 109) or add some sautéed greens, a salad or fermented veg on the side.

- 600 g chicken livers
- 3 tablespoons coconut oil or other good-quality fat*
- 1 teaspoon ground turmeric
- ¼ teaspoon ground cumin
- 1 onion, finely diced
- 1 tablespoon finely grated ginger
- 185 g (¾ cup) canned diced tomatoes
- 125 ml (½ cup) Chicken Bone Broth (see recipe, page 256)
- 1 tablespoon fish sauce
- ¼ teaspoon chilli powder (optional)
- coriander leaves, to serve
- sea salt and freshly ground black pepper

** See Setting Up Your Paleo Kitchen*

Rinse the chicken livers under cold water, pat dry with paper towel and trim off any fat, sinew and veins. Set aside.

Place a wok or large frying pan over medium heat. Add the oil or fat and when it is hot, add the turmeric and cumin and stir constantly for 10 seconds. Immediately add the onion and cook, stirring occasionally, for 5 minutes until the onion is soft and translucent. Turn the heat down to medium–low, add the ginger and tomatoes and simmer for 6 minutes, stirring occasionally.

Tilt the pan slightly and push the sauce to one side. Increase the heat to medium–high, add the chicken livers and seal for 1 minute on each side until brown. Push the sauce back to the centre of the pan and gently mix with the livers. Add the bone broth, bring to the boil, then turn back down to a simmer. Stir through the fish sauce and chilli powder (if using) and cook for a further 2–3 minutes until the chicken livers are just cooked through. Sprinkle with coriander leaves, season with salt and pepper and serve.

SERVES 4

Roasted paprika chicken

I adore playing around with old favourites like the humble roast chook. This is a simple yet flavoursome recipe – you really need to make it to understand how a smattering of spices can elevate a roast chicken to such a memorable dish. As always, double or even triple the recipe so that you have lots of meat leftover for breakfast and lunch the next day – you could enjoy it with eggs in the morning, or shred the meat and add veggies to create a salad or stir-fry.

- 4 chicken marylands (about 1 kg in total)
- sea salt and freshly ground black pepper
- juice of 1 lemon
- 2 tablespoons coconut oil or other good-quality fat*, melted
- 1½ teaspoons coriander seeds, crushed
- 1½ teaspoons smoked paprika
- 2 tablespoons balsamic vinegar
- 2 garlic cloves, crushed
- 3 baby fennel bulbs, cut into wedges
- 2 carrots, cut in half lengthways
- 1 large onion, cut into wedges
- 1 lemon, cut into wedges
- 125 ml (½ cup) Chicken Bone Broth (see recipe, page 256) or water
- ¼ bunch of kale (about 100 g), central stalks removed and leaves torn
- Cauliflower Puree (see recipe, page 186), to serve

** See Setting Up Your Paleo Kitchen*

Season the chicken with salt and pepper, place in a large bowl and set aside.

In another bowl, to make the marinade, combine the lemon juice, oil or fat, coriander seeds, smoked paprika, balsamic vinegar and garlic, then mix well.

Pour the marinade over the chicken and rub into the skin. Cover with plastic wrap and place in the fridge for 1 hour to marinate.

Preheat the oven to 200°C.

Arrange the fennel, carrot, onion and lemon wedges in a single layer in a roasting tin. Season with salt and pepper and place the marinated chicken on top, then pour over the marinade and bone broth or water. Roast in the oven, occasionally basting the chicken with the juices in the tin, for 35–40 minutes until the chicken is cooked through and golden. About 8 minutes before the chicken is ready, gently toss in the kale, mixing it with the juices in the tin to ensure it is well covered and will not dry out and burn. Add a little more salt and pepper, if desired. Serve the roast chicken with cauliflower puree or other accompaniments of your choice.

SERVES 4

Cauliflower fried rice with greens and sriracha

Cauliflower fried rice is a favourite for many who have gone paleo, as it takes less than 20 minutes to make, is cheap and flavoursome, and you can customise it depending on what you have in the fridge.

- 1 head of cauliflower (about 1 kg), separated into florets
- 4 slices of bacon, diced
- 3 tablespoons coconut oil or other good-quality fat *
- ½ onion, finely chopped
- 2 garlic cloves, crushed
- 100 g shiitake or oyster mushrooms, sliced
- 2.5-cm piece of ginger, finely grated
- 100 g fresh okra *, sliced
- ½ bok choy, shredded
- ¼ bunch of Chinese broccoli (gai larn) (about 150 g), chopped
- 2½ tablespoons tamari
- 50 g bean sprouts
- 2 spring onions, finely sliced
- 2 tablespoons chopped coriander leaves
- 2 tablespoons chopped flat-leaf parsley leaves
- 1 large handful of water spinach (see note), roughly chopped
- sea salt and freshly ground white pepper
- 4–6 eggs

To serve

- coriander leaves
- sesame seeds, toasted
- fish sauce
- lime wedges
- Paleo Sriracha Chilli Sauce (see recipe, page 249)
- Kimchi (see recipe, page 110)

** See Setting Up Your Paleo Kitchen*

Note

Water spinach is also known as morning glory. It's popular in many South-East Asian countries and is available from Asian grocers.

Place the cauliflower in the bowl of a food processor and pulse until it resembles rice.

Fry the bacon in a large frying pan or wok over high heat until crispy. Remove and set aside.

Heat 2 tablespoons of the oil or fat in the same pan over high heat, add the onion and garlic and cook for a few minutes, or until softened. Stir in the mushrooms and ginger and cook for another few minutes. Stir in the okra, bok choy and Chinese broccoli and cook for 2 minutes. Add the cauliflower and stir-fry for 2–3 minutes, or until tender. Add the bacon, tamari, sprouts, spring onion, herbs, water spinach and some salt and pepper and cook for 1–2 minutes, or until everything is heated through and well combined. Remove from the pan and keep warm.

Wipe the pan clean and place over medium–high heat. Add the remaining oil or fat and swirl it around in the pan. Crack one egg into the centre, shake the pan gently to prevent the egg from sticking, and fry for 1–2 minutes until the egg is cooked to your liking. Carefully lift out the egg with a spatula, place on a plate and keep warm. Repeat with the remaining eggs, adding a little more oil if needed.

Serve the cauliflower rice garnished with some coriander leaves, sesame seeds, a splash of fish sauce and a squeeze of lime. Top with the fried eggs, then drizzle with some sriracha and serve with a bowl of kimchi to pass around the table.

SERVES 4–6

Pork and garlic stuffed mushrooms

This dish was created by twins Monica and Jacinta Cannataci, who are two of my closest friends and colleagues. Mon and Jac have been working side by side with me for more than a decade; they are accomplished chefs and the ones responsible for making my recipes look so freaking good in these photos! I asked the girls to submit a recipe for this book and this is what they came up with. I've gotta say it is an absolute winner, so thank you girls. I look forward to supporting you both over coming decades in seeing you achieve your dreams.

- 12 large field mushrooms
- 2 tablespoons coconut oil or other good-quality fat*, melted

Italian sausage stuffing

- 500 g pork mince
- 3 cloves Confit Garlic (see below), crushed
- 1 teaspoon dried chilli flakes
- 1½ teaspoons fennel seeds, toasted and coarsely ground
- 1¼ teaspoons sea salt
- ½ teaspoon freshly ground black pepper
- 2 tablespoons tallow or pork lard
- 1 tablespoon chopped flat-leaf parsley leaves, plus extra to serve
- 1 red capsicum, roasted, peeled, deseeded and diced

Confit garlic

- 25 garlic cloves (about 100 g), peeled
- 250 ml (1 cup) coconut oil

** See Setting Up Your Paleo Kitchen*

To make the confit garlic, place the garlic and oil in a saucepan over very low heat (do not allow the oil to boil). Gently poach for 1 hour, or until the garlic is beautifully soft. Transfer the garlic and oil to a sterilised glass jar, seal and store in the fridge for up to 3 months.

Remove and finely chop the mushroom stems and reserve them for the sausage stuffing.

To make the sausage stuffing, mix all the ingredients with the finely chopped mushroom stems in a bowl until well combined. Set aside.

Preheat the oven to 190°C.

Lightly grease the base of a shallow baking dish and arrange the mushroom caps, gill-side up, in a single layer. Divide the sausage stuffing between the mushroom caps and drizzle with a good amount of oil or fat. Season with salt and pepper. Cover with foil and bake for 15 minutes, remove the foil and bake for a further 10 minutes until the mushrooms are deep golden brown. Sprinkle on the extra chopped parsley and serve with a green salad or some raw cauliflower tabouli (see recipe, page 124).

SERVES 4

TIP

The leftover confit garlic can be used to make a simple and delicious aioli (see recipe, page 250).

Pork cutlets with romesco sauce and cabbage slaw

Let me share a little secret with you: sauces and dressings are the key to taking your cooking from good to extraordinary. I've included a whole chapter on dressings and sauces (see pages 237–253) and I urge you to try making some of them. I always have a couple of homemade sauces in the fridge to liven up my dishes. The sauce used in this dish is a classic Spanish romesco, which is made from roasted capsicums and hazelnuts, vinegar, garlic, extra-virgin olive oil and smoked paprika. It is amazing teamed with pork, but is delicious dolloped onto fried eggs and asparagus too. I also love to pop some wild prawns on the barbecue then smother them with romesco and eat them, shell and all. Or you could try romesco with grilled fish, squid skewers, scallops ... you get the picture!

- 125 ml (½ cup) extra-virgin olive oil
- 4 tablespoons apple cider vinegar
- ¼ savoy cabbage (about 450 g)
- 200 g brussels sprouts
- 150 g almonds (activated if possible, see page 198), toasted and chopped
- 1 handful of flat-leaf parsley leaves, finely chopped
- 1 handful of mint leaves, finely chopped
- sea salt and freshly ground black pepper
- 4 pork cutlets (about 300 g each), pounded with a mallet until 2-cm thick
- 2 tablespoons coconut oil or other good-quality fat*, melted
- 125 ml (½ cup) Romesco Sauce (see recipe, page 243)

** See Setting Up Your Paleo Kitchen*

Whisk the olive oil and vinegar in a bowl to make a simple vinaigrette and set side.

Discard the outer leaves of the cabbage. Finely shave the cabbage and brussels sprouts with a sharp knife or mandoline, discarding any thick ribs from the cabbage. Combine the cabbage and brussels sprouts in a large bowl and add the almonds, parsley and mint. Add half of the vinaigrette, season with salt and pepper, then toss together gently. Allow the salad to stand for up to 10 minutes.

Meanwhile, coat the pork chops with the coconut oil or fat and season with salt and pepper. Heat a frying pan over medium–high heat and cook the pork chops for 4 minutes on each side until cooked through. Remove from the heat and allow to rest for 2 minutes.

Spread the romesco sauce evenly on four serving plates. Top with a pork chop and some of the salad and serve.

SERVES 4

Balinese roast pork belly

This dish is based on the classic Indonesian dish *babi guling*, which is usually made with a whole suckling pig. The spice paste is sensational and can be used to flavour a roast chicken or other meat. Enjoy the leftovers with eggs for breakfast or heated in chicken broth with some veggies for dinner.

- 2 kg boned pork belly, skin left on
- 2 tablespoons coconut oil or other good-quality fat*, melted
- ½ tablespoon sea salt
- 4 kaffir lime leaves, finely shredded
- 4 curry leaves, finely shredded

Spice mix

- 1 teaspoon sea salt
- 4 garlic cloves, crushed
- 2-cm piece of ginger, roughly chopped
- 100 g fresh turmeric, grated
- 6 bird's eye chillies, deseeded and finely chopped
- 6 French shallots, finely chopped
- 4 kaffir lime leaves, finely shredded
- 4 fresh curry leaves, finely shredded
- 2 lemongrass stems, white part only, bruised and finely chopped
- 1½ tablespoons coriander seeds, crushed
- 3 tablespoons coconut oil or other good-quality fat*, melted
- 1 tablespoon black peppercorns, finely crushed
- 2-cm piece of fresh galangal (see note), coarsely chopped

To serve

- steamed Asian greens (try water spinach, bok choy or Chinese broccoli)
- lime wedges

** See Setting Up Your Paleo Kitchen*

Note

Galangal is similar in appearance to ginger and has a distinct peppery flavour. It's available from Asian grocers and some supermarkets.

Gently pour 250 ml of boiling water over the pork belly skin, then pat the pork skin and meat dry with paper towel. Discard the water. Drizzle 1 tablespoon of the oil or other fat over the skin and rub in the salt, making sure that the skin is covered evenly. Set aside.

To make the spice mix, process all the ingredients in a food processor to a fine paste. Heat the remaining oil or fat in a frying pan over medium heat. Add the spice paste and fry for 3 minutes, stirring constantly, until fragrant. Remove from the heat and allow to cool.

Place the pork, skin-side down, on a chopping board. Spread a layer of the spice paste over the belly flesh, then scatter the shredded lime and curry leaves over the paste evenly. Starting with one of the long sides, carefully roll the pork belly to form a tight roll. Tie the roll tightly with kitchen string at five even intervals. Cover and refrigerate for at least 1 hour for the flavours to infuse (leave overnight for best results).

Preheat the oven to 220°C. Remove the pork from the fridge and allow to come to room temperature.

Transfer the pork to a wire rack set in a roasting tin and roast for 30 minutes, or until the skin starts to crackle. Reduce the temperature to 180°C and continue to roast, basting occasionally, for a further 1–1½ hours until the pork is cooked (the juices will run clear when the thickest part is pierced with a skewer). Rest for 15 minutes before carving into thick slices. Serve with Asian greens and lime wedges.

SERVES 6

Homemade merguez sausages

It's actually really easy to make your own sausages, and also reassuring to know exactly what has gone in them. These days, most meat in sausages is poor quality and comes from inhumanely raised animals. Many store-bought sausages also contain various fillers and preservatives. These little merguez sausages may not look quite as perfect as store-bought ones, but they will taste so much better. Merguez sausages are from North Africa and they do have a little kick to them from the harissa. Play around with different herbs and spices to suit your taste and feel free to use chicken, pork or beef mince instead of lamb. You will need to start this recipe a day ahead.

- 400 g lean lamb mince
- 100 g lamb fat, chopped (see note)
- 1 tablespoon harissa (see note)
- 1 teaspoon ground cinnamon
- 3 garlic cloves, crushed
- ¼ teaspoon crushed fennel seeds
- 1 teaspoon dried mint leaves
- 1 teaspoon sea salt

Note

You should be able to source a piece of lamb fat from your butcher. Harissa is a North African paste made from chillies, paprika and olive oil. It's available from supermarkets and specialty food stores.

Combine the lamb mince, fat, harissa, cinnamon, garlic, fennel seeds, mint and salt together in a bowl and knead for 5 minutes. Cover and place in the refrigerator overnight to marinate.

Heat the barbecue to medium. Form the lamb mixture into sausage shapes and cook for 8–10 minutes, turning occasionally, until cooked through. Serve with a simple salad of tomato, red onion wedges and pickled red onion, or with any of the salads in the salads and vegetables chapter (see pages 107–135).

SERVES 4

Lamb moussaka

The key to going paleo is to make food that the whole family will enjoy and that will last a day or two. This moussaka fits the bill perfectly – it is bursting with flavour and will easily keep in the fridge for a few days. Serve with a Greek salad (minus the cheese) and some sauerkraut (see recipe, page 121).

- 1 large eggplant (about 450 g), sliced 1-cm thick
- sea salt
- 4 tablespoons coconut oil, melted
- ½ bunch of silverbeet or kale (about 200 g), central stalks removed and leaves chopped
- 2 onions, chopped
- 4 garlic cloves, crushed
- 600 g lamb or beef mince
- 1 teaspoon ground cinnamon
- freshly ground black pepper
- 160 g tomato paste
- 310 ml (1¼ cups) Beef or Chicken Bone Broth (see recipes, pages 258 and 256) or water
- 50–100 g offal (such as marrow, heart, liver)
- 3 tablespoons chopped flat-leaf parsley leaves

Cauliflower white sauce

- ½ head cauliflower (about 550 g), cut into florets
- 500 ml (2 cups) coconut milk
- 3 tablespoons arrowroot (see note)
- 1 egg

Note

Arrowroot is a gluten-free starch made from the roots of the tapioca and cassava plants. You'll find it at supermarkets and health food stores.

Preheat the oven to 180°C.

Generously salt both sides of the eggplant slices and leave for 1 hour (this draws out excess moisture and stops the eggplant becoming bitter and watery). Rinse under cold water and pat dry with paper towel. Brush the eggplant with about 1 tablespoon of the melted coconut oil and cook in batches in a frying pan over high heat until lightly browned. Remove from the pan and set aside. Wipe the pan clean, then add another tablespoon of the coconut oil and sauté the silverbeet or kale over medium heat for 2 minutes or until wilted. Remove from the pan and set aside.

Melt the remaining coconut oil in the frying pan over medium heat. Add the onion and garlic and cook for 5 minutes, or until softened. Stir in the lamb or beef mince and cinnamon, breaking up any lumps with a spatula. Season with salt and pepper and cook until the meat is browned. Add the tomato paste and bone broth or water, mix to combine and simmer for 15 minutes. Stir through the offal and remove from the heat.

Meanwhile, to make the cauliflower white sauce, steam the cauliflower for 15 minutes until very soft. Pour half of the coconut milk into a saucepan and bring to the boil. Mix the arrowroot with the remaining coconut milk until combined. When the milk has boiled, turn the heat down to low and whisk in the coconut and arrowroot mixture. Cook, whisking constantly, for 1 minute until the sauce has thickened. Remove from the heat and whisk in the egg, then stir in the cauliflower. Transfer the cauliflower mixture to a food processor and process until smooth and creamy. Season with salt and pepper and allow to cool slightly.

To assemble, lay half the eggplant slices in a single layer in a large baking dish. Spread the silverbeet or kale on top, then pour on the mince mixture. Add the remaining eggplant slices then sprinkle over the parsley. Finally, pour over the cauliflower white sauce.

Bake for 40 minutes, or until lightly golden. Allow to stand for 15 minutes before cutting and serving with a simple green salad.

SERVES 6

Lamb meatballs with pumpkin and pomegranate

This is an awesome recipe for getting kids involved – whether it's measuring out the spices, peeling the garlic, mixing the ingredients or rolling the meatballs. Make a double batch of the meatball mix and the next morning, pan-fry some of the leftover mix, crack in a few eggs and bake in the oven!

- 500 g lamb mince
- 1 garlic clove, crushed
- 1 tomato, deseeded and diced
- 1 tablespoon pomegranate molasses, plus extra to serve
- 2 tablespoons coconut oil or other good-quality fat*

Turkish spice mix

- 4 tablespoons ground cumin
- 3 tablespoons dried mint
- 3 tablespoons dried oregano
- 2 tablespoons sweet paprika
- 2 teaspoons hot paprika
- 2 tablespoons freshly ground black pepper

Roast pumpkin

- ½ kent pumpkin (about 1.4 kg), cut into 2.5-cm wedges
- 2 tablespoons coconut oil, melted
- sea salt and freshly ground black pepper
- 2 pinches of ground cumin

Tahini sauce

- 120 g (½ cup) unhulled tahini
- 1 tablespoon lemon juice
- 1 teaspoon ground sumac*
- ½ teaspoon ground cumin
- 1 small handful of mint leaves, chopped

To serve

- extra-virgin olive oil
- ground sumac*
- pumpkin seeds (activated if possible, see page 198)
- seeds of 1 pomegranate
- mint leaves
- lemon wedges

** See Setting Up Your Paleo Kitchen*

To make the Turkish spice mix, place all the ingredients in an airtight container and shake well to combine.

Preheat the oven to 200°C.

To make the roast pumpkin, place the pumpkin wedges on a baking tray, drizzle with the coconut oil and toss to coat evenly. Arrange the pumpkin in a single layer, season with salt and pepper and sprinkle on the cumin. Roast for 20–25 minutes until tender.

Meanwhile, combine the lamb with the garlic, tomato, 1½ tablespoons of the Turkish spice mix and the pomegranate molasses in a bowl. Mix thoroughly and season with salt and pepper. Coat a baking tray with 1 tablespoon of coconut oil or fat. Shape the lamb mixture into walnut-sized meatballs. Heat the remaining coconut oil or fat in a large frying pan over medium heat. Pan-fry the meatballs for 2–3 minutes until browned. Transfer to the prepared tray in a single layer and bake until cooked through, about 5 minutes.

To make the tahini sauce, combine the tahini, 4 tablespoons of water, the lemon juice, sumac, cumin and mint in a bowl and stir until smooth.

To serve, place the roasted pumpkin on a serving platter, drizzle with a little olive oil, season with salt and pepper and sprinkle on the sumac, pumpkin seeds, pomegranate seeds and mint. Finish with a drizzle of the tahini sauce. Transfer the meatballs to a serving bowl and drizzle on some extra pomegranate molasses. Serve with the remaining tahini sauce and the lemon wedges alongside.

SERVES 4

Thai beef mince with fried eggs

Although this recipe is in the main meals chapter – and it does make a brilliant mid-week dinner – I actually often eat it for breakfast! Regardless of when you decide to cook this, the key is creating a lovely umami flavour through the addition of sugar-free fish sauce. And the runny egg yolk creates a sauce of its own that is just too damn good to refuse. Serve sautéed Asian greens or a fresh salad on the side. Leftovers can be packed into kids' lunchboxes with lettuce or cabbage cups and cucumber chunks.

- 3 tablespoons coconut oil or other good-quality fat*, plus more if needed
- 2 eggs
- 2 small red chillies, sliced
- 3 garlic cloves, crushed
- 300 g beef mince
- 125 ml (½ cup) Chicken Bone Broth (see recipe, page 256)
- 1 tablespoon fish sauce, or to taste
- 1 tablespoon tamari or coconut aminos* (optional)
- 1 teaspoon honey (optional)
- ¼ teaspoon Chinese five spice
- 2 large handfuls of Thai basil leaves
- sea salt and freshly ground black pepper

Hot and sour sauce

- 4 tablespoons fish sauce
- juice of 2 limes
- 2–4 bird's eye chillies, finely sliced (depending on how hot you like it)
- 1 garlic clove, crushed
- 1 teaspoon grated ginger
- 1 teaspoon honey (optional)
- coriander leaves, chopped (optional)

** See Setting Up Your Paleo Kitchen*

To make the hot and sour sauce, combine the fish sauce, lime juice, chilli, garlic, ginger and honey (if using) in a small bowl, mix well and set aside. For best results, make this at least 1 hour or up to 1 day in advance; the longer you leave it, the stronger the sauce will be.

Heat a wok or large frying pan over medium–high heat. Add 1 tablespoon of oil or fat and swirl it around in the pan. Crack one egg into the centre and fry, shaking the pan gently to prevent the egg from sticking, until cooked to your liking, 1–2 minutes. Carefully lift out the egg with a spatula, place on a plate and keep warm. Repeat with the other egg, adding a little more oil if needed.

Return the pan to high heat. Add the remaining oil or fat and swirl it around in the pan. Stir in the chilli and garlic and cook until fragrant, 1 minute. Add the beef and stir-fry until brown, 2 minutes. Pour in the bone broth and simmer for 3 minutes. Mix in the fish sauce, tamari or coconut aminos (if using), honey (if using) and Chinese five spice. Toss in the basil and as soon as it wilts, remove the pan from the heat. Season to taste with salt and pepper.

To serve, divide the mince between two serving plates and top each with a warm fried egg. Sprinkle the coriander on the hot and sour sauce (if using) and spoon the sauce over the eggs.

SERVES 2

Meatballs with tomato and bone marrow sauce

Simple recipes like this are the key to a paleo lifestyle. We are not reinventing the wheel here; instead, we're going back to a time when food was real and simple. If you can't find any beef liver, lamb liver will work just as well.

- 100 g beef liver
- 100 g beef heart
- 4 tablespoons coconut oil or other good-quality fat*
- 2 handfuls of baby spinach or kale leaves
- 2 garlic cloves, finely chopped
- 2 French shallots, finely chopped
- 350 g pork mince
- 150 g beef mince
- 2 tablespoons chopped flat-leaf parsley leaves
- 1 egg
- 2 tablespoons almond meal
- ¼ teaspoon dried chilli flakes (optional)
- sea salt and freshly ground black pepper
- baby basil leaves, to serve

Tomato sauce

- 800 g beef marrow bones, cut into 5-cm pieces (ask your butcher to do this)
- 2 tablespoons coconut oil or other good-quality fat*
- 3 garlic cloves, finely sliced
- 500 g canned crushed tomatoes
- 8 basil leaves
- sea salt and freshly ground black pepper

** See Setting Up Your Paleo Kitchen*

To make the tomato sauce, pop the marrow out of the bones, slice the marrow into 5-mm thick pieces and set aside. Heat the oil or fat in a saucepan over medium heat, add the garlic and fry until lightly browned. Add the tomatoes and 125 ml of water and simmer for 20–25 minutes. Add the basil and simmer for a further 5 minutes. Season with salt and pepper.

Preheat the oven to 180°C.

Use your fingers to remove the membranes from the liver and heart, then cut out any little tubes with a small sharp knife. Finely chop the liver and heart and set aside.

Heat 1 tablespoon of oil or fat in a frying pan over medium heat. Add the spinach or kale and cook until just wilted. Remove the pan from the heat, drain and squeeze out any excess liquid from the spinach or kale, then roughly chop. Set aside to cool.

Return the pan to medium heat and add another tablespoon of oil or fat and the garlic and shallot. Fry for 3 minutes, or until the shallot is translucent and the garlic is lightly browned. Set aside.

In a large bowl, mix the pork mince, beef mince, liver, heart, spinach or kale, garlic, shallot, parsley, egg, almond meal, chilli flakes (if using) and some salt and pepper until well incorporated. Place the bowl in the fridge for 30 minutes so that the meat cools a little and will be easier to roll.

Once cool, roll the mixture into golf ball–sized portions. Heat the remaining oil or fat in a large ovenproof frying pan and fry the meatballs (in batches if necessary) until golden on one side. Turn over and place the pan in the oven for 5 minutes until the meatballs are cooked through.

Add the tomato sauce and sliced bone marrow to the meatballs in the pan, cover with a lid and heat gently on the stovetop until ready to serve.

Sprinkle with the basil leaves and serve.

SERVES 4

Pepper beef hotpot

This hotpot is a mid-winter winner if ever I have tasted one. All you need is some well-sourced ingredients and a few hours to allow them to simmer on the stovetop so that their flavours intensify and deepen. I have kept it simple by just adding pumpkin and silverbeet, but feel free to add in any other veggies that you love – okra, zucchini, cauliflower, broccoli, Jerusalem artichoke and mushrooms are all great.

- 1 × 1 kg beef shoulder, cut into 3-cm cubes
- 1 teaspoon sea salt
- 2 tablespoons coconut oil or other good-quality fat*
- 4 garlic cloves, finely chopped
- 2 onions, chopped
- 2 carrots, chopped
- 2 celery stalks, chopped
- 1–2 long red chillis, deseeded and finely chopped, plus extra sliced chilli to serve
- 2 spring onions, chopped
- 1.5 litres (6 cups) Beef or Chicken Bone Broth (see recipes, pages 258 and 256)
- 1 teaspoon ground allspice
- ½ tablespoon freshly ground black pepper, plus more to taste
- 1 teaspoon thyme leaves
- 2 bay leaves
- 500 g pumpkin, peeled and cut into 2.5-cm cubes
- 3 silverbeet leaves, trimmed and torn

** See Setting Up Your Paleo Kitchen*

Place the beef cubes in a bowl, rub with the salt and let sit at room temperature for 30 minutes.

Melt the oil or fat in a very large saucepan over medium–high heat. Working in batches, add the beef cubes and seal on all sides. Remove the beef from the pan and set aside. To the same pan, add the garlic, onion, carrot, celery and chilli and cook until softened, about 5 minutes. Add the spring onion and cook for 2 minutes. Add the beef back to the pan along with the bone broth, allspice, pepper, thyme and bay leaves and bring to the boil. Reduce the heat to low and simmer gently for at least 2 hours until the meat is starting to become tender (do not allow to boil or the beef will become tough). Add the pumpkin and continue to cook for 20 minutes until both the beef and pumpkin are completely tender. Stir in the silverbeet and cook until wilted, about 5 minutes. Season with salt and pepper.

Spoon into bowls, scatter over some sliced chilli and serve.

SERVES 6

Shepherd's pie

This shepherd's pie is probably not that different to the one that your grandmother might have made – except that I have swapped the potato for cauliflower. This is the kind of real food that people used to eat – and the return to wholesome, unprocessed food is the basis of the paleo lifestyle. Our great grandparents probably would have also put livers, hearts, marrow or brains in there – please try adding one of these if you're feeling brave! Offal is so nutrient dense and you may find that you love the flavour.

- 2 tablespoons coconut oil or other good-quality fat*
- 1 teaspoon ground cumin
- 1 onion, diced
- 4 garlic cloves, crushed
- 2 celery stalks, diced
- 2 carrots, diced
- 600 g beef or lamb mince
- 2 lamb brains, soaked in cold water with 1 teaspoon salt for 1 hour, rinsed well and finely chopped (optional)
- 2½ tablespoons tomato paste
- 1 teaspoon chopped thyme leaves
- 4 tablespoons dry red wine (such as shiraz) (optional)
- 375 ml (1½ cups) Beef or Chicken Bone Broth (see recipes, pages 258 and 256)
- sea salt and freshly ground black pepper
- 3 tablespoons roughly chopped flat-leaf parsley leaves

Cauliflower puree

- 1 large head of cauliflower (about 1.3 kg), chopped into florets
- 2 tablespoons coconut oil, melted
- sea salt and freshly ground black pepper

** See Setting Up Your Paleo Kitchen*

To make the cauliflower puree, fill a large saucepan with water and bring to the boil, then add the cauliflower and cook until tender, about 10 minutes. Drain in a colander and set aside to cool slightly. Place the cooled cauliflower in a food processor and process until smooth. Add the the oil and puree, then season with salt and pepper.

Preheat the oven to 180°C.

Heat the oil or fat in a large, deep frying pan over medium–high heat. Add the cumin, onion, garlic, celery and carrot and cook for 5 minutes, or until the vegetables are softened and beginning to brown. Add the mince and brains (if using) and cook, stirring to break up any lumps, until browned. Add the tomato paste and thyme and cook for 1 minute, then pour in the wine (if using) and bone broth and simmer for 10 minutes, stirring occasionally. Season with salt and pepper.

To assemble, spread the meat mixture into the base of an ovenproof dish and level with a spoon. Cover with the cauliflower puree and smooth the top out evenly. Bake for 30 minutes, or until the top is lightly golden. Sprinkle with the parsley and serve with a fresh salad of your choice.

SERVES 6

Bolognese on sautéed kale

Bolognese is a hit for all ages. Make up a big batch and use the leftovers to make bolognese muffins – simply mix in a few eggs, spoon into muffin trays and bake!

- 2 tablespoons coconut oil or other good-quality fat*
- ½ onion, chopped
- ½ carrot, finely diced
- ½ celery stalk, finely diced
- 3 garlic cloves, crushed
- 550 g beef mince
- 1 teaspoon chopped oregano leaves
- 200 ml dry red wine (such as shiraz)
- 2 tablespoons tomato paste
- 500 g tomato passata
- 300 ml Chicken or Beef Bone Broth (see recipes, pages 256 and 258)
- pinch of dried chilli flakes (optional)
- sea salt and freshly ground black pepper
- 50–100 g offal (such as marrow, heart or liver)
- 4 tablespoons finely chopped flat-leaf parsley leaves

Sautéed kale

- 3 tablespoons coconut oil
- 3 garlic cloves, crushed
- 2 bunches of kale (about 800 g), central stalks removed and leaves torn
- 125 ml (½ cup) Chicken Bone Broth (see recipe, page 256)

Paleo parmesan

- 70 g macadamia nuts (activated if possible, see page 198), finely chopped
- 1 tablespoon flat-leaf parsley leaves, finely chopped
- 1 salted anchovy fillet, rinsed, patted dry and finely chopped
- 1 tablespoon extra-virgin olive oil
- finely grated zest of ½ lemon
- pinch of sea salt

** See Setting Up Your Paleo Kitchen*

Preheat the oven to 150°C. Line a baking tray with baking paper.

To make the paleo parmesan, combine all the ingredients in a bowl and mix well. Spread the mixture on the prepared tray and bake for 5–8 minutes, or until lightly golden. Set aside to cool.

Heat the oil or fat in a large frying pan over medium–high heat. Add the onion, carrot and celery and cook for 4–5 minutes, or until softened. Next, add the garlic and cook for 1 minute, or until fragrant. Add the mince and brown, breaking up the meat into smaller pieces with a spoon, for 5–6 minutes. Stir in the oregano and wine and cook until the wine has almost evaporated, about 4–5 minutes. Add the tomato paste and cook for 1 minute, then stir in the passata, half the bone broth, the chilli flakes (if using) and season with salt and pepper. Reduce the heat to low and simmer for 15 minutes. Add the rest of the broth if it becomes too dry. Stir through the offal and parsley and keep warm.

To prepare the kale, heat a large frying pan over medium–high heat, add the oil and garlic and cook, stirring, until fragrant, about 30 seconds. Add the kale and bone broth and cook, tossing occasionally, for 3 minutes until wilted. Season with salt and pepper.

Divide the kale between four bowls and top with the bolognese and paleo parmesan.

SERVES 4

Barbecued sirloin with mushrooms, horseradish and rocket

As a kid, mum would cook a steak for me every week or two and I looked forward to it each and every time. Not a lot has changed since then, except perhaps that I am more picky about where my meat comes from and what cuts I choose to cook with. As always, search out quality grass-fed beef from a trusted source and choose your cut depending on preference and budget. Some of my favourite cuts are hanger, bavette, rib eye and sirloin. I have teamed the steak with a simple accompaniment of sautéed mushrooms with horseradish and rocket. Remember to include a spoon of fermented vegetables on the side; and if you really want to take it to the next level, serve it with some roasted bone marrow – heavenly!

- 4 × 200 g sirloin steaks
- 2 tablespoons coconut oil or other good-quality fat*, melted
- sea salt and freshly ground black pepper
- 150 g Swiss brown mushrooms, sliced
- 100 g oyster mushrooms, sliced
- 2 garlic cloves, crushed
- 3 thyme sprigs, chopped
- 1 tablespoon chopped flat-leaf parsley leaves
- 2 handfuls of wild rocket
- 3 tablespoons extra-virgin olive oil or macadamia oil
- 2 lemons, cut into wedges
- 1 tablespoon grated fresh horseradish

** See Setting Up Your Paleo Kitchen*

Preheat a barbecue to hot. Coat the steaks with a little of the coconut oil or fat and season with salt and pepper. Cook the steaks on one side for 2–3 minutes, then flip over and cook for another 2–3 minutes, or until cooked to your liking. Remove from the heat, place on a plate and cover with foil. Allow to rest for 4–6 minutes in a warm place.

Meanwhile, heat the remaining coconut oil or fat in a frying pan over high heat, add the mushrooms, garlic and thyme and sauté until the mushrooms are cooked through, 2–4 minutes. Season with salt and pepper, stir in the parsley, then remove from the heat and cover to keep warm.

Toss the rocket with the olive or macadamia oil and a squeeze of lemon juice and season with salt and pepper.

Once the steaks have rested, return them to a very hot barbecue and cook for 30 seconds on each side to make sure they are warm. Place each steak on a serving plate, then sprinkle with the horseradish.

Serve the steaks with the dressed rocket, sautéed mushrooms and lemon wedges.

SERVES 4

Spiced roast beef

Like many Australian families, we try to do a roast on Sunday every week. Not only is it lovely to spend time preparing and eating it together, but it also means that we have heaps of leftovers for the start of the week. The leftovers might become a roast beef, rocket and boiled egg salad, a beef and vegetable soup or simply a roast beef sandwich with paleo bread (see recipe, page 200).

- 100 ml coconut oil or other good-quality fat*, melted
- sea salt and freshly ground black pepper
- 1 × 1.2 kg rolled and tied scotch fillet, boneless beef rib-eye, sirloin or rump
- 3 parsnips, cut in half lengthways
- 4 thyme sprigs
- ½ bunch of kale (about 200 g), central stalks removed

Spice rub

- 1 tablespoon coconut oil or other good-quality fat*, melted
- 3 garlic cloves, crushed
- 60 g coriander seeds, crushed
- 2 tablespoons freshly ground black pepper
- ½ teaspoons dried chilli flakes (optional)

** See Setting Up Your Paleo Kitchen*

Preheat the oven to 160°C.

To make the spice rub, combine all of the ingredients in a small bowl.

Rub 2 tablespoons of the oil and a generous pinch of salt into the beef, then rub with the spice mix until evenly coated.

Heat 2 tablespoons of the oil in a large roasting tin over high heat and sear the beef, turning occasionally, for 5 minutes, or until well browned on all sides. Remove the beef from the roasting tin and add the parsnip and thyme, in a single layer. Place the beef on top and pour 250 ml of water into the tin. Roast for 60 minutes for medium–rare (55–60°C on a meat thermometer). For medium, roast the beef for a further 5 minutes (63–66°C on the meat thermometer). If you like your meat well done, continue to roast the beef for a further 10–15 minutes, or until the temperature reaches 69–74°C. Transfer the roast beef to a carving tray, cover loosely with foil and allow to rest for 15 minutes.

Heat the remaining oil in a frying pan over medium heat. Add the kale and sauté for 3 minutes, or until cooked through and slightly wilted. Season with salt and pepper.

Carve the meat and serve with the roasted parsnip and sautéed kale.

SERVES 6

ST GERMAIN

SNACKS

Hard-boiled eggs

It might seem crazy to include this as a recipe, but a boiled egg is pretty much the healthiest and most satisfying snack ever in my opinion! Rich in protein and good fats, an egg or two will fill you up and stop you from snacking on unhealthier options. I recommend boiling up a dozen or so eggs at a time, depending on how many people there are in your family. Keep them in the fridge for snacks or to chop up and add to salads (they will last in the fridge for 7 days unpeeled or 5 days peeled). If you want to get fancy you can slice some truffle over your eggs, team them with some caviar or roll them in finely chopped activated nuts and seeds (see recipe, page 198). For me, all it takes is salt, pepper, dried chilli flakes and some chopped herbs and I am a happy man.

4 eggs

Bring a small saucepan of water to the boil over high heat. Reduce the heat to low so that the water is simmering, then add the eggs and cook for 7 minutes. Drain and, when cool enough to handle, peel the eggs under cold running water. Cut each egg in half and serve.

SERVES 2

Spiced activated nuts and seeds

Nuts and seeds are a delicious and nutritious addition to a paleo-inspired way of life. It is important to purchase the best organic nuts and seeds you can find and to properly prepare them by soaking and then rinsing – otherwise known as 'activating' them. You can eat them as is after soaking and rinsing, but I like to add spices and dehydrate them in a very low oven or dehydrator, which makes them lovely and crunchy. You can use pretty much any nut or seed in this recipe – see the box below for the different lengths of time they'll need to be soaked for.

500 g nuts (such as almonds, brazil nuts, cashew nuts, hazelnuts, macadamia nuts, pecans, pistachio nuts or walnuts) or seeds (such as pumpkin or sunflower seeds)

1 teaspoon spice or spice blend (such as cayenne pepper, smoked paprika, ground cumin, ground turmeric or curry powder) (optional)

sea salt

Place the nuts or seeds in a bowl, add enough filtered water to cover, then set aside to soak for the required time (see box).

After soaking, the nuts and seeds will look nice and puffy and may even start to show signs of sprouting. Rinse the nuts and seeds under running water. Drain well and pat dry with paper towel.

Spread the nuts and seeds onto a large baking tray and sprinkle over the spice or spice blend (if using) and some salt. Slowly dry out the nuts and seeds in a dehydrator or on the lowest temperature in your oven (around 50°C). This will take anywhere from 6–24 hours. The nuts and seeds are ready when they feel and taste dry. They last really well in an airtight container kept at room temperature for up to a couple of months.

MAKES 500 G

SOAKING TIMES

- Almonds, brazil nuts and hazelnuts: 12 hours
- Macadamia nuts: 7–12 hours
- Walnuts: 4–8 hours
- Pecans and pistachios: 4–6 hours
- Cashew nuts: 2–4 hours
- Pumpkin seeds: 7–10 hours
- Sunflower seeds: 2 hours

PETES
NUTS

Nic's paleo bread

When my wife Nic and I first posted the recipe for this bread, my Facebook page almost went into meltdown. This tasty and really simple loaf is free of wheat, grain, gluten, refined sugar and toxic oils. It is a fabulous alternative if you are really hooked on grain-based bread, and is perfect with some marinated olives (see recipe, page 204) or alongside your eggs for breakfast. Just keep in mind that it's probably not a good idea to eat it daily, especially if you are trying to lose weight. It is still a bit of a 'filler' – the more of this you consume, the fewer veggies and good-quality protein you'll be eating.

- 100 g (1 cup) almond meal, sifted
- 50 g (½ cup) coconut flour, sifted
- 4 tablespoons psyllium husk powder*
- 2 teaspoons baking powder
- 8 eggs, beaten until fluffy
- 1 tablespoon apple cider vinegar
- 4 tablespoons extra-virgin olive oil
- 1 tablespoon dried mixed herbs (optional)
- a few good pinches of sea salt and freshly ground black pepper

** See Setting Up Your Paleo Kitchen*

Set the oven to 120°C. Grease a loaf tin and line the base and sides with baking paper, cutting into the corners to fit.

Combine all the dry ingredients in a bowl, then add the beaten egg, vinegar, olive oil, herbs (if using) and salt and pepper and stir well to combine. Scoop the mixture into the prepared tin and spread out evenly. Bake for 80 minutes, or until a skewer inserted into the bread comes out clean. Remove from the oven, allow to cool a little in the tin, then turn out onto a wire rack. Slice and eat with whatever tickles your fancy. We love to dip this bread into olive oil, coconut aminos and homemade dukkah.

MAKES 1 LOAF

Tip

I like to use the Wild For Life Still Earth blend of thyme, parsley, sage, rosemary, bay leaf, garlic and black pepper in this recipe.

OPINEL

Curried macadamia kale chips

If you have never made or eaten kale chips, please give this recipe a try. Get your kids to help you tear the leaves off the kale stalks and massage the coconut oil into them to coat. Then add some curry powder and macadamias and I can guarantee you they will be eating their greens faster than you ever imagined. Feel free to play around with the spices to suit your taste. Cumin, cayenne pepper and sumac are all fabulous too.

- 60 g macadamia nuts, soaked overnight in filtered water
- 3 tablespoons coconut oil
- 1 tablespoon lemon juice
- ¼ teaspoon sea salt
- 1 large bunch of kale (about 400 g), central stalks removed, leaves roughly torn
- 1½ teaspoons curry powder

Preheat the oven to 120°C. Grease and line a large baking tray with baking paper.

Drain the macadamia nuts and pat dry with paper towel. Combine the nuts, coconut oil, lemon juice and salt in the bowl of a food processor and process to make a slightly coarse paste. (Alternatively, use a mortar and pestle to crush the nuts, then add the remaining ingredients and pound to form a coarse paste.) Transfer the paste to a large bowl, add the kale and toss to coat evenly. Season with more salt if you like and sprinkle over the curry powder.

Arrange the kale in a single layer on the prepared tray and bake for 30–40 minutes. Don't overcook the chips or they'll burn! Remove from the oven and cool on the baking tray.

SERVES 2–4

Marinated olives with garlic and thyme

I talk a lot about good fats in this book, and olives are an excellent way to up your intake. They are high in mono-unsaturated fats (the same fats found in avocados), which can improve blood cholesterol levels and reduce the risk of heart disease. These marinated olives are wonderful on their own but can also be added to any number of dishes to make them shine – roast chicken, grilled wild-caught fish or a simple but gorgeous summer salad of tomatoes and basil.

- 2 teaspoons fennel seeds
- 2 teaspoons coriander seeds
- 300 g mixed olives, with or without pits, your choice
- zest of 2 lemons, sliced into 1-cm strips
- 1 teaspoon sea salt
- ½ teaspoon freshly ground black pepper
- 200 ml olive oil
- 3 tablespoons sherry vinegar
- 2 garlic cloves, crushed
- large pinch of dried chilli flakes
- 6 sprigs of thyme
- 4 bay leaves

Combine the fennel and coriander seeds in a frying pan and toast over medium heat, shaking the pan often to evenly distribute the spices, for 1–2 minutes, or until fragrant.

Place the olives, lemon zest, salt, pepper, oil, vinegar, garlic, chilli flakes, thyme and bay leaves in a bowl, add the toasted seeds and mix well. Cover and marinate for at least 1 hour or, for best results, overnight in the refrigerator.

Transfer the olives and marinade to a saucepan and gently warm over low heat for 3–5 minutes. (Don't allow the oil to go over 100°C.) Serve warm, with a little bowl for the pits if needed.

SERVES 4

Macadamia cheese

We steer clear of dairy when following a paleo way of eating as it can cause major digestive issues; however, many people find it very difficult to give up cheese. I get it. I was a cheese lover for as long as I can remember and it was really tough for me to let go of it, but when I discovered nut cheeses it became a lot easier. Nut cheeses, such as this macadamia version, can be used in place of normal cheese in lots of different ways. Put a bowl of it out with some celery and carrot sticks or paleo bread (see recipe, page 200) when friends pop over or dollop it on top of bolognese (see recipe, page 189).

- 320 g macadamia nuts
- 1 tablespoon lemon juice
- 1 teaspoon sea salt
- pinch of freshly ground black pepper

Soak the macadamias in 750 ml of filtered water for at least 7 hours – overnight is best. Drain and rinse the nuts thoroughly under warm water.

Place the macadamias in the bowl of a food processor and add the lemon juice and salt and pepper, then pulse for 1 minute to combine. Add 240 ml of water and process until smooth. If the macadamia cheese seems overly thick or dry, gradually add more water and lemon juice to adjust the consistency. The macadamia cheese can be stored in an airtight container in the refrigerator for up to 1 week.

MAKES 600 G

VARIATIONS

Cashew nuts can be used in place of the macadamias – simply soak the cashew nuts for 2–4 hours and halve the amount of water added when processing.

You can also add other flavours – try 1 teaspoon of truffle oil or chilli oil.

Celery boats with herbed chicken salad

Celery is one of the most understated vegetables I reckon. Chefs use it in so many preparations as it is part of the *mirepoix*: a mix of onion, carrot and celery that forms the basis of most French stocks and sauces. Celery is also sensational raw, in terms of both flavour and texture. Topping this beautiful vegetable with a simple chicken salad that has been mixed with creamy homemade mayonnaise is surely one of life's little luxuries. And the kids will love 'em too!

- 6 wide celery stalks, trimmed
- sea salt and freshly ground black pepper

Chicken salad

- 4 tablespoons Mayonnaise (see recipe, page 250)
- 1½ tablespoons lemon juice, plus extra if desired
- 1 tablespoon finely chopped chervil leaves, plus extra to garnish
- 1 teaspoon finely chopped tarragon leaves
- 1 tablespoon finely chopped flat-leaf parsley leaves
- 1 teaspoon finely grated lemon zest
- 300 g cooked chicken thigh fillets, finely chopped or shredded
- ½ red onion, finely chopped

Using a vegetable peeler, peel the rounded part of the celery stalks so they sit flat, then cut them into 4-cm lengths.

To make the chicken salad, place the ingredients in a bowl and mix until combined.

Season the chicken salad with salt and pepper, taste and add a little more lemon juice if desired.

Spoon the chicken salad into the celery boats, place on a platter and garnish with a few extra chervil leaves.

SERVES 4

Bacon guacamole with plantain crisps

If I was trapped on a desert island and I got one wish I would have to choose an avocado tree. This fruit is one of the true wonders of nature. They are high in mono-unsaturated fats, which our bodies absolutely thrive on. They lower your risk of heart disease and stroke and provide nutrients that assist in maintaining your body's cells. I usually eat about half an avocado a day and some of my favourite ways are on the side of my eggs for breakfast, in a smoothie (see recipe, page 232), diced and added to the top of a curry, and in this incredibly simple guacamole. I have served this dip with crispy plantains, which are a low-sugar variety of banana that needs to be cooked to be eaten. If you don't have access to plantains, you could serve it with sticks of celery, fennel and carrot instead.

- 2 green plantains
- 2 tablespoons coconut oil, melted
- sea salt and freshly ground black pepper

Bacon guacamole

- 1 teaspoon coconut oil
- 70 g bacon, finely diced
- 1½ avocados, diced
- 1 green chilli, deseeded and finely chopped (optional)
- juice of 1 lime or more to taste
- 1–2 tablespoons finely diced red onion
- 2 tablespoons chopped coriander leaves
- 1 tablespoon extra-virgin olive oil

Preheat the oven to 180°C. Grease and line a large baking tray with baking paper.

Trim both ends of the plantains, then thinly cut them lengthways using a mandoline or sharp knife. Trim and remove the green skin on the edges of each slice.

Place the plantain strips in a single layer on the prepared tray, making sure that the strips are not touching. Brush the plantain strips with the oil and sprinkle on some salt. Transfer to the oven and bake, turning the tray once for even cooking, for 10 minutes until the plantain strips are lightly golden and crisp. Keep a close eye on them to prevent the plantain from burning. Set aside to cool completely.

To make the bacon guacamole, melt the coconut oil in a frying pan over medium heat, add the bacon and cook, stirring occasionally, for 4–6 minutes until golden and crispy. Transfer the crispy bacon to paper towel to soak up any excess oil. Allow to cool completely. Combine the bacon with all the remaining ingredients in a small bowl and gently mix. Season with salt and pepper to taste.

Serve the guacamole straight away with the plantain crisps and maybe some chopped raw veg, too, if you wish.

SERVES 4

Snags with sauerkraut and tomato ketchup

Is it a snack; is it a meal; is it a breakfast? I don't really know, but this dish is going to leave you feeling good at any time of day. We get our sausages from a great butcher who uses free-range pigs and makes the snags in the old-fashioned way using only meat, fat, spices and seasonings. We usually buy 40 or so at a time and get them divided into packets of about 6–8 snags, which we'll pop in the freezer. I usually pull out a pack or two just before the weekend and cook them up on a Saturday morning. We have some with our brekkie, then the rest go into the fridge to be eaten as a snack with some cultured veg.

- 1 tablespoon coconut oil or other good-quality fat*
- 4 gourmet sausages of your choice
- sea salt and freshly ground black pepper
- Sauerkraut with Dill and Juniper Berries (see recipe, page 121), to serve
- Tomato Ketchup (see recipe, page 252), to serve
- Fermented Mustard (see recipe, page 238), to serve

** See Setting Up Your Paleo Kitchen*

Heat the oil or fat in a large heavy-based frying pan over medium–high heat, add the sausages, reduce the heat to medium, and cook, turning occasionally, for 8–10 minutes until cooked through. Season with salt and pepper.

Cut each sausage lengthways without going all the way through and slightly open up to create a cavity. Fill the cavity with a heaped tablespoon of sauerkraut and spread it out evenly. Squeeze over some tomato ketchup and mustard and serve.

SERVES 4

Tuna and bacon cucumber boats

I am always looking for fun ways to get more greens into the kids' diets, and these cucumber boats are one of my favourites of recent times. To be honest, I often just grab a cucumber from the fridge when I am heading out the door to eat in the car or on the plane. It does the job for me, being low in sugar and high in water and nutrients. I find after I eat a whole cucumber then I am sweet for a while. But I couldn't just put a cucumber in the book as a recipe, so I thought I would jazz it up with a simple tuna and bacon salad!

- coconut oil, for frying
- 3 slices of bacon, finely diced
- 1 avocado, chopped
- juice of ½ lemon, plus extra if desired
- 1 tablespoon avocado oil or extra-virgin olive oil
- 3 tablespoons chopped flat-leaf parsley leaves
- ½ celery stalk, finely diced
- 300 g canned tuna, in brine or olive oil, drained
- 2 spring onions, finely sliced, plus extra to garnish
- sea salt and freshly ground black pepper
- 2 Lebanese cucumbers

Heat a little coconut oil in a frying pan over medium–high heat, add the bacon and cook for 4–5 minutes until crispy and golden. Strain out the excess fat and allow the bacon to cool.

Mash the avocado with a fork until creamy but still slightly chunky, then mix in the lemon juice, avocado or extra-virgin olive oil, parsley, celery, tuna, bacon (reserving about 1 tablespoon to garnish) and spring onion until well combined. Season with salt and pepper. Add a little more lemon juice, if desired.

To make the cucumber boats, cut the cucumbers into 5-cm pieces, then halve lengthways and, using a teaspoon, scoop out and discard the seeds, leaving the flesh and skin intact.

Fill each cucumber boat with the avocado and tuna, and garnish with a little extra sliced spring onion and the reserved bacon.

SERVES 4

FOOD

DRINKS

Daily bone broth with turmeric, cumin and lemon

I have a vision for the future and it involves everyone drinking bone broths daily instead of coffee! I know you might be wondering whether I have totally lost the plot, but I think we need to do something to help our modern-day health problems and one of the best ways to start is by healing the gut. Bone broths do just that and are also pretty damn delicious. This recipe is infused with turmeric as well as some lemon juice to alkalise your system. Drink a cup a day!

350 ml hot Fish, Chicken or Beef Bone Broth (see recipes, pages 255, 256 and 258)

1 teaspoon ground turmeric

pinch of ground cumin

2 teaspoons lemon juice, or to taste

sea salt

Pour the hot broth into a large mug. Add the turmeric, cumin, lemon juice and a pinch of salt and give it a good stir. Take a sip and enjoy at any time of day.

SERVES 1

Lemon water

This is the single most important recipe in this whole book – clean filtered water! I drink at least 2 litres of water a day and I always start with at least 500 ml during the first 10–20 minutes after I wake up, as that is when our bodies are most dehydrated. Room temperature water is ideal because it doesn't shock your system too much. Adding a little lemon juice or raw apple cider vinegar has a much-needed alkalising effect on the body (despite the fact that both are acidic). I really recommend installing a good filtration system at home to remove unwanted chemicals from your water. There are some affordable domestic filtration systems on the market these days and while it might seem like a big investment initially, when you think about how much water you consume, it is definitely worth it. My other suggestions for drinking water are pretty simple. First, invest in a good-quality re-usable water bottle so that you can fill it up before you leave home and don't have to buy bottled water and contribute to landfill. Second, don't drink water with your meals, as it can wash away the digestive enzymes that are needed to break down your food. Finally, don't drink just before going to bed – you want to maximise restful sleep by avoiding waking up in the middle of the night to go to the bathroom. So, drink in the morning and between meals; limit drinking after dinner; and aim for at least 2 litres a day depending on how physically active you are and how hot the weather is. Easy!

1 litre (4 cups) room temperature or lukewarm filtered water

juice of 1 lemon or 2 tablespoons apple cider vinegar

Stir the water and lemon juice or apple cider vinegar together and drink, on an empty stomach, in the first 30 minutes upon waking. Food or other drinks should not be consumed until at least 30–60 minutes later.

SERVES 1

Ginger and licorice iced tea

I don't drink coffee as it is a stimulant that can mess with your adrenal system. Anything that stimulates you is also likely to make you crash a little later, which means you feel the need for something else to pick you up again. This is exactly the kind of rollercoaster ride we are trying to avoid by following a paleo way of eating. Skipping coffee doesn't mean you have to miss out altogether though. This licorice and ginger iced tea is an amazing way to begin your day – ginger is fabulous for digestion and the licorice gives the drink a slightly sweet flavour, without actually being full of sugar. You can also experiment with different spices mixes in this tea; you could even jar them up and give them to friends and family as a gift.

- 4 tablespoons licorice root sticks*, broken into pieces
- 2.5-cm piece of ginger, sliced or grated
- 1 cinnamon stick
- 1 small handful of mint leaves
- juice of 1 lemon (optional)
- ice cubes

** See Setting Up Your Paleo Kitchen*

Put the licorice root, ginger and cinnamon in a large teapot and pour in 1 litre of boiling water. Allow to steep for 20 minutes.

Pour the tea through a fine strainer into a jug. Add the mint and lemon (if using) and stir. Let cool to room temperature, then cover and chill in the refrigerator.

Strain and serve with ice cubes. (Of course, the tea can be served hot, too! Simply steep for 3–5 minutes before serving.)

SERVES 2–4

Green juice with ginger and lime

Green juices are, of course, so much better for you than a soft drink or energy drink as you can get a whole heap of nutrients in a single glass. On the down side, however, you are missing out on all of the amazing fibre in the veggies by juicing them. While I definitely do drink green juices like this from time to time, I still consider them a bit of a treat. Another important thing to note is that, unlike a smoothie, a green juice is never going to be able to replace a meal as it doesn't have enough protein and fibre to keep you full. So, if you are juicing in the morning, make sure you include some healthy dietary fat in your breakfast (see recipes, pages 88–105) to make sure you are not starving by 9am.

½ bunch of kale (about 200 g)

2 large handfuls of baby or English spinach leaves

4 celery stalks

2 Lebanese cucumbers

1 lime, peeled

2 handfuls of flat-leaf parsley leaves

1 handful of mint leaves

10-cm piece of ginger

1 green apple, chopped

1 tablespoon green superfood powder (see note) (optional)

Note

Green superfood powders contain a blend of powdered algae and green vegetables, providing a concentrated hit of antioxidants, vitamins and minerals. They are available from health food stores and pharmacies.

Combine all the ingredients except the superfood powder (if using) in a juicer and juice together. Stir in the superfood powder. Pour into two tall glasses and serve immediately.

SERVES 2

Nut milk

Many people, especially those who grew up in a home where milk was a part of the daily routine, find that substituting nut milk for cow's milk makes the transition to paleo a lot easier. Nut milk is so simple to make – it is basically just nuts that have been soaked in water, rinsed, blended and strained. You can use the leftover solids to make paleo bread (see recipe, page 200) or to add into smoothies to thicken them up. As for the milk, you can use it in all of the ways that cow's milk is used. Try it on paleo muesli (see recipe, page 101), in chai tea, to make ice cream, in smoothies or just on its own as a treat.

1 cup activated almonds, macadamia nuts or walnuts (see recipe, page 198)

1 litre (4 cups) filtered water

Place the nuts in a blender, add the water and blend for a couple of minutes until smooth.

Line a bowl with a piece of muslin so that the muslin hangs over the rim. Pour the blended nuts and water into the bowl. Pick up the edges of the muslin, bring together and twist to squeeze out all the milk. (The leftover solids can be used to make bliss balls or in baking recipes in place of almond meal.)

Pour the nut milk into a sterilised 1-litre jar or bottle, cover and place in the fridge. Give it a good shake when you want to use it. Nut milk will last, stored in the refrigerator, for 3–4 days.

MAKES 1 LITRE

Turmeric and coconut kefir

Kefir is one of the easiest fermented drinks to make and you only have to wait 36 hours for it to ferment before bottling and popping it in the fridge. I like to use young coconut water for my kefir and have added fresh turmeric to this as it is a natural anti-inflammatory and powerful antioxidant.

3 young coconuts*

2 tablespoons water kefir grains or 2 probiotic capsules (see note)

1½ tablespoons finely grated fresh turmeric

* *See Setting Up Your Paleo Kitchen*

Note

Probiotic capsules contain live bacteria and are available at health food stores and pharmacies. Water kefir grains are small, gelatinous colonies of bacteria and yeast used to make fermented drinks. You can buy them from some health food stores or online.

You will need a 750-ml glass jar for this recipe. Wash the jar and a non-metal spoon in hot soapy water, then run them through the dishwasher on a hot rinse cycle to sterilise. Alternatively, place the jar and spoon in a large saucepan filled with water and boil for 10 minutes. Put on a baking tray in a 150°C oven to dry.

Open the coconuts by cutting off the tops. Strain the coconut water into your sterilised jar. If using a probiotic capsule, open up the capsule. Add the probiotic powder or water kefir grains to the coconut water, then add the turmeric and, using the sterilised spoon, stir well. Cover with a clean piece of muslin and rubber band. Place in the pantry or a dark spot for 24–48 hours to let it ferment. Your kefir is ready when the water turns from relatively clear to cloudy white.

Taste test after 24–30 hours. Pour some kefir into a glass – it should taste sour, with no sweetness left, like coconut beer. Some batches are fizzier than others. If it still tastes sweet, place it back in the pantry for the remaining recommended fermentation time. Once you're happy with the flavour, pour through a sieve to remove the water kefir grains (if using) and return the kefir to the jar. Keep in the fridge for up to 2 months. The water kefir grains can be stored in coconut water in the fridge until you make your next batch of kefir (refresh the coconut water every 5 days or so).

SERVES 2

Tips

- It's important to sterilise all materials that come into contact with the kefir. You just want to grow good bacteria, not bad, so boil everything in hot water and be sure to wash your hands well.
- Glass jars and storage bottles are preferable to plastic since kefir eats away at plastic, which means that you will end up eating plastic. Limited contact is fine, but prolonged is discouraged.
- Only use coconut water from young coconuts. Packaged coconut water won't work because it is pasteurised.
- Never add probiotics to cold water as it will drastically slow the fermentation process.

Avocado, coconut and mint smoothie

Going paleo is all about embracing good-quality fats. Avocados, coconuts, nuts, seeds and eggs are just some of the wonderful sources of the healthy fats that our bodies need to thrive. Try having one of these bad boys (or should I say good guys) for breakfast one day a week and just see how you feel for the next 3–4 hours. Play around with different herbs and spices – whatever takes your fancy. You can also try freezing any leftover smoothie mix into popsicle moulds for a treat on a hot day – the kids will love it!

1 young coconut*

½ avocado, stone and skin removed

1 large handful of silverbeet or other greens, central stalks removed and leaves roughly chopped

1 small handful of mint leaves

80 ml (⅓ cup) Nut Milk (see recipe, page 226) or coconut milk

2 eggs

1 tablespoon coconut oil

1–2 teaspoons gelatine or collagen powder (ideally from grass-fed cattle)

3 walnuts, soaked for 2 hours then drained

3 macadamia nuts, soaked for 2 hours then drained

½ teaspoon ground cinnamon

1 vanilla pod, split and seeds scraped

** See Setting Up Your Paleo Kitchen*

Open the top of the coconut and pour the coconut water into the jug of a blender. Scoop the coconut flesh out of the shell and roughly chop.

Combine the coconut flesh and the remaining ingredients with the coconut water in the blender and blend until smooth. Serve immediately.

SERVES 2

Tips

- If you can't find a young coconut, feel free to replace the flesh and coconut water with 150 ml of coconut water and 3 tablespoons of desiccated coconut.
- You can pre-soak the nuts and store them in an airtight container in the fridge for up to 4 days.

1000

FOOD
THE NEW

Creamy chai smoothie

This is an awesome smoothie that gets some of the most powerful spices into your diet in a very simple way. I love that you can whip up a drink like this in less than 5 minutes and it will fill you up. You could also add avocado if you want it even thicker and creamier, or chia seeds for added texture and fibre, or even sumac for a touch of citrus. Take your time drinking a smoothie like this – it's pretty much a meal in itself so it's good to go slowly and give your body a chance to digest it all properly.

- 1 teaspoon ground cinnamon, plus extra to serve
- ½ teaspoon ground cardamom
- ½ teaspoon ground cloves
- 1 teaspoon finely grated ginger
- 2 teaspoons finely grated fresh turmeric or 1 teaspoon ground turmeric
- 2 eggs
- 1 tablespoon coconut oil
- 1–2 teaspoons gelatine or collagen powder (ideally from grass-fed cattle)
- 20 macadamia nuts, soaked for 2 hours then drained
- 250 ml (1 cup) coconut water
- 250 ml (1 cup) coconut cream or coconut milk

Place all the ingredients in a blender and blend until smooth. Pour into glasses, dust with a pinch of extra cinnamon and serve immediately.

SERVES 2

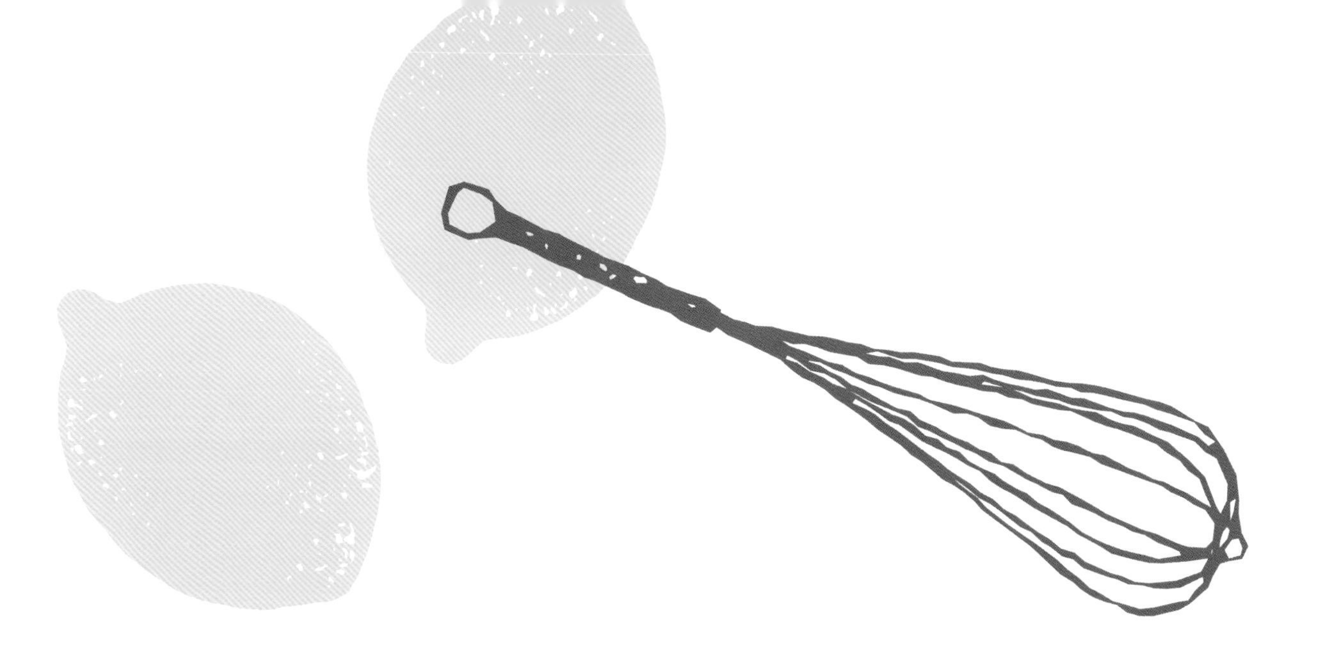

DRESSINGS, SAUCES *and* BROTHS

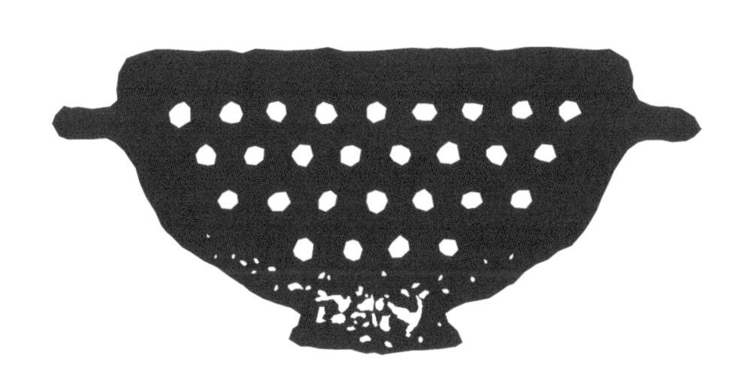

Mustard vinaigrette

- 4 tablespoons apple cider vinegar or lemon juice
- 2 tablespoons Fermented Mustard (see recipe below) or wholegrain mustard
- 1 teaspoon sea salt
- ¼ teaspoon freshly ground black pepper
- 1 garlic clove, crushed
- 250 ml (1 cup) extra-virgin olive oil or macadamia oil

Combine all of the ingredients in a screw-top jar, cover and shake well. Store in the refrigerator for up to 2 weeks. Shake well before using.

MAKES 400 ML

Fermented mustard

- 185 ml sauerkraut brine (see recipe, page 121, or use a store-bought sauerkraut)
- 80 g brown and yellow mustard seeds (brown are hotter and will make a spicier mustard)
- 1 French shallot
- 2 garlic cloves
- 1 tablespoon maple syrup
- sea salt

You will need a 250-ml preserving jar with airlock lid. Wash the jar and your utensils thoroughly in very hot water or run them through a hot rinse cycle in the dishwasher.

Combine the sauerkraut brine, mustard seeds, shallot and garlic in a glass or stainless steel bowl, cover with a plate and allow to soak at room temperature overnight.

The next day, combine the soaked seed mixture with the maple syrup in a food processor. If you like lots of whole seeds in your mustard, you'll only need to process for 30 seconds or so; if you like a smoother mustard, process for longer until you reach your desired texture. Add salt to taste.

Store in the preserving jar in the fridge for up to 3 months.

MAKES 250 ML

Herb vinaigrette

125 ml (½ cup) extra-virgin olive oil

3 tablespoons apple cider vinegar

2 tablespoons finely chopped mixed herbs (such as chervil, flat-leaf parsley, dill and tarragon)

1 garlic clove, crushed

pinch of sea salt

Combine all the ingredients in a screw-top jar and season with salt. Cover and shake well. Serve immediately or store in the refrigerator for up to 3 days. Shake well before using.

MAKES 185 ML

Green goddess dressing

½ avocado

3 tablespoons coconut milk

3 tablespoons lemon juice

1 garlic clove, crushed

2 anchovy fillets, finely chopped

4 tablespoons flat-leaf parsley leaves

3 tablespoons chopped basil leaves

1 tablespoon chopped tarragon leaves

¼ teaspoon sea salt

125 ml (½ cup) extra-virgin olive oil

Place all the ingredients except the oil in a food processor and process until well combined. With the motor running, slowly pour in the oil and process until the dressing thickens and the herbs are finely chopped. Transfer to a bowl, cover and refrigerate until ready to serve. Store in an airtight container in the fridge for up to 4 days or in the freezer for 3 months.

MAKES 250 ML

Nam jim dressing

- 4 red Asian shallots, chopped
- 2 long red chillies, deseeded and chopped
- 2 garlic cloves, chopped
- 2.5-cm piece of ginger, peeled and chopped
- 1 teaspoon chopped coriander root
- 150 ml lime juice
- 2½ tablespoons fish sauce

Pound the shallots, chillies, garlic, ginger and coriander root using a mortar and pestle to form a paste. Add the lime juice and mix well. Add the fish sauce. Taste and adjust the seasoning if necessary so that the dressing is a balance of hot, sour, salty and sweet.

Strain through a sieve and discard the pulp. Store in a glass jar in the fridge for 3–4 weeks.

MAKES ABOUT 200 ML

Bacon and sherry vinaigrette

- 1 tablespoon coconut oil
- ½ French shallot, finely chopped
- 120 g bacon, finely diced
- 4 tablespoons sherry vinegar or apple cider vinegar
- 1 teaspoon Fermented Mustard (see recipe, page 238) or Dijon mustard
- 1 teaspoon finely snipped chives
- 100 ml extra-virgin olive oil
- sea salt and freshly ground black pepper

Heat half of the coconut oil in a small saucepan over low heat, add the shallot and cook for 5 minutes, until soft. Remove from the pan. Add the remaining coconut oil and the bacon to the pan and fry over medium heat, stirring occasionally, for 6–8 minutes, or until golden. Add the vinegar and shallot and set aside to cool.

Transfer the bacon and shallot mixture to a bowl and whisk in the mustard, chives and olive oil and season with salt and pepper. Store in a glass jar in the fridge for up to 1 week.

MAKES ABOUT 250 ML

Romesco sauce

- 2 red capsicums, quartered
- 2 tomatoes, quartered
- 1 long red chilli, deseeded and chopped
- 1 teaspoon smoked paprika
- 1 sprig of rosemary, leaves picked and finely chopped
- 1 tablespoon coconut oil, melted
- sea salt and freshly ground black pepper
- 12 hazelnuts (activated if possible, see page 198), lightly toasted
- 12 almonds (activated if possible, see page 198), lightly toasted
- 3 garlic cloves, crushed
- 2 tablespoons apple cider vinegar
- 4 tablespoons extra-virgin olive oil

Preheat the oven to 220°C. Place the capsicum, skin-side up, on a tray and bake for 10–15 minutes, or until the skin blackens. Place the capsicum in a bowl, cover with plastic wrap and set aside for 5 minutes. Peel off the skin and remove the seeds, then chop the flesh and set aside.

Toss the tomato, chilli, paprika, rosemary and coconut oil in a bowl and season with salt and pepper. Heat a chargrill pan over high heat, add the tomato mixture and cook for 3–4 minutes until soft. Peel the tomato quarters and chop.

Place the nuts in a food processor and process until finely ground. Add the capsicum, tomato and chilli mixture, garlic and vinegar and process to a paste. With the motor running, slowly add the olive oil and process until well combined. Taste and add more salt and pepper if necessary.

The romesco sauce can be stored in an airtight container in the fridge for up to 1 week.

MAKES ABOUT 400 G

My favourite ways to use romesco sauce:

- dolloped on top of grilled seafood
- alongside pork cutlets (see recipe, page 171)
- as a snack with vegetable sticks for dipping
- whisked into salad dressings for a chilli kick

Beetroot chimichurri

- 1 large beetroot (about 200 g), peeled and grated
- 250 ml (1 cup) extra-virgin olive oil, plus extra as needed
- 1 large handful of flat-leaf parsley leaves
- ½ red onion, chopped
- 2 garlic cloves, crushed
- 4 tablespoons chopped oregano leaves
- 4 tablespoons apple cider vinegar
- ½ teaspoon dried chilli flakes
- sea salt and freshly ground black pepper

Combine the grated beetroot, oil, parsley, onion, garlic, oregano, vinegar and chilli flakes in the bowl of a food processer and pulse until finely chopped. Add a little more oil if the sauce is too thick.

Season with salt and pepper and serve. Store in an airtight container in the fridge for up to 1 week.

MAKES ABOUT 600 G

Try using beetroot chimichurri in these delicious ways:

- serve it alongside any good-quality protein, such as meat, chicken, fish or even game – I think the earthy flavour of the beetroot goes particularly well with game
- use it to generously coat large cubes of venison, leave to marinate for an hour or so, then thread the cubes onto skewers and pop them straight on the barbecue
- serve it as a dip alongside fresh vegetable sticks and paleo bread (see recipe, page 200)

Salsa verde

- 250 ml (1 cup) extra-virgin olive oil
- 2 handfuls of basil leaves
- 2 handfuls of mint leaves
- 2 handfuls of flat-leaf parsley leaves
- 2 garlic cloves, chopped
- 4 anchovy fillets
- 50 g salted baby capers, rinsed well and patted dry
- 1 tablespoon finely chopped cornichons (optional)
- 1 tablespoon lemon juice
- 50 g (⅓ cup) pine nuts, toasted
- sea salt and freshly ground black pepper

Combine all the ingredients in the bowl of a food processor and blitz to form a thick paste.

Keep the salsa verde in a glass jar in the fridge for up to 1 week.

MAKES ABOUT 500 G

Top tips for using salsa verde:

- serve it alongside grilled wild fish or meat
- stir it through some homemade aioli (see recipe, page 250) and serve as a dipping sauce for chicken nuggets or sweet potato fries
- dollop it on top of a bowl of creamy chicken and cabbage salad (see recipe, page 153) for an extra boost of flavour
- toss it through a bowl of zucchini noodles (see recipe, page 154) and sprinkle over some paleo parmesan (see recipe, page 189) for the perfect quick meal

CHILLI

Paleo sriracha chilli sauce

- 680 g long red chillies or jalapeno chillies, deseeded and roughly chopped
- 8 garlic cloves, crushed
- 4 tablespoons apple cider vinegar
- 3 tablespoons tomato paste
- 1 large medjool date, pitted
- 2 tablespoons fish sauce
- 1½ teaspoons sea salt

Combine all the ingredients in the bowl of a food processor and process until smooth.

Pour the chilli mixture into a saucepan and bring to the boil over high heat, stirring occasionally to prevent the chilli from burning on the base of the pan. As soon as it comes to the boil, reduce the heat to low and simmer, stirring occasionally, for 5–10 minutes. At this point the sauce will become vibrant and red. Remove from the heat and allow to cool.

Transfer the sriracha to a large glass jar, cover and refrigerate until needed. It will keep for up to 2 weeks in the fridge.

MAKES 625 G

THANK YOU ...

To Nom Nom Paleo for sharing their amazing homemade sriracha recipe. It is so full of flavour with none of the nasty stuff. I particularly love serving it with Asian-style eggs (see recipe, page 95) and cauliflower fried rice (see recipe, page 166).

Mayonnaise

- 4 egg yolks
- 2 teaspoons Dijon mustard
- 2 teaspoons apple cider vinegar
- 2 tablespoons lemon juice
- 400 ml olive oil
- salt and freshly ground black pepper

Place the egg yolks, mustard, vinegar and lemon juice in a food processor and process for 30 seconds to combine.

With the motor running, slowly pour in the oil in a thin stream and process until thick and creamy. Season with salt and pepper.

Leftover mayonnaise can be stored in an airtight container in the fridge for up to 5 days.

MAKES ABOUT 500 G

Aioli

To make aioli instead, simply add 4 confit garlic cloves (see recipe, page 168) to the food processor along with the egg yolks, mustard, vinegar and lemon juice and proceed with the recipe as above.

Tomato ketchup

180 g tomato paste
1 tablespoon apple cider vinegar
1 teaspoon garlic powder
1 teaspoon onion powder
1 teaspoon ground cinnamon
¼ teaspoon freshly grated nutmeg
1 teaspoon honey (optional)
⅛ teaspoon ground cloves

Combine the tomato paste and 4 tablespoons of water in a small saucepan over medium heat and bring to a simmer. Remove from the heat and stir in the remaining ingredients until fully incorporated. (Add more water if you'd prefer a thinner sauce.)

Allow the sauce to cool, then pour into a glass jar or container, cover and store in the refrigerator for 2–4 weeks.

MAKES ABOUT 300 ML

Fish bone broth

- 2 tablespoons coconut oil
- 1 garlic bulb, cut in half horizontally
- 1 leek, rinsed well and roughly chopped
- 2 celery stalks, roughly chopped
- 2 onions, roughly chopped
- 1 carrot, roughly chopped
- 125 ml (½ cup) dry white wine or vermouth (optional)
- 3 or 4 whole fish carcasses including heads (such as snapper, barramundi, kingfish)
- 3 tablespoons apple cider vinegar
- several thyme sprigs
- several flat-leaf parsley stalks
- 1 dried bay leaf
- 1 teaspoon black peppercorns
- 1 lemon, halved

Melt the oil in a stockpot or large saucepan over medium–low heat. Add the garlic and vegetables and cook very gently for 30 minutes, or until soft. Pour in the wine or vermouth (if using) and bring to the boil. Add the fish carcasses and cover with 3 litres of cold water. Stir in the vinegar and bring to the boil, skimming off the scum and impurities as they rise to the top.

Tie the herbs together with kitchen string and add to the pan with the peppercorns and lemon. Reduce the heat to low, cover and simmer for 6 hours.

Remove the carcasses with tongs or a slotted spoon and strain the liquid into storage containers for the refrigerator or freezer. Chill well in the refrigerator and remove any congealed fat before placing in the fridge or the freezer for long-term storage. The broth can be stored in the refrigerator for up to 3–4 days or frozen for up to 3 months.

MAKES 2.5 LITRES

Chicken bone broth

- 1–1.5 kg bony chicken parts (such as necks, backs, breastbones and wings)
- 2–4 chicken feet (optional)
- 2 tablespoons apple cider vinegar
- 1 large onion, roughly chopped
- 2 carrots, roughly chopped
- 3 celery stalks, roughly chopped
- 2 leeks, white part only, rinsed well and roughly chopped
- 1 garlic bulb, cut in half horizontally
- 1 tablespoon black peppercorns, lightly crushed
- 2 bay leaves
- 2 large handfuls of flat-leaf parsley stalks

Place the chicken pieces in a stockpot or large saucepan, add 5 litres of cold water, the vinegar, onion, carrot, celery, leek, garlic, peppercorns and bay leaves and let stand for 1 hour to help draw out the nutrients from the bones.

Place the stockpot or pan over medium–high heat and bring to the boil, skimming off the skin that forms on the surface of the liquid. Reduce the heat to low and simmer for 12–24 hours. The longer you cook the broth the richer and more flavourful it will be. About 10 minutes before the broth is ready, add the parsley.

Strain the broth through a fine sieve into a large storage container, cover and refrigerate until the fat rises to the top and congeals. Skim off this fat and store the broth in airtight containers in your refrigerator or freezer. The broth can be stored in the refrigerator for 3–4 days or frozen for up to 3 months.

MAKES 3.5 LITRES

Tip

Farm-raised, free-range chickens will give the best results. Many battery-raised chickens will not produce broth that sets.

Beef bone broth

- about 2 kg beef knuckle and marrow bones
- 1 cow's foot, cut into pieces (optional)
- 3 tablespoons apple cider vinegar
- 1.5 kg meaty beef rib or neck bones
- 3 onions, roughly chopped
- 3 carrots, roughly chopped
- 3 celery stalks, roughly chopped
- 2 leeks, white part only, rinsed well and roughly chopped
- 3 sprigs of thyme
- 2 bay leaves
- 1 teaspoon black peppercorns, crushed
- 1 garlic bulb, cut in half horizontally
- 2 large handfuls of flat-leaf parsley stalks

Place the knuckle and marrow bones and cow's foot (if using) in a stockpot or very large saucepan, add the vinegar and pour in 5 litres of cold water, or enough to cover. Let stand for 1 hour to help draw out the nutrients from the bones. Remove the bones from the water, reserving the water.

Preheat the oven to 180°C.

Place the knuckle and marrow bones, cow's foot (if using) and meaty bones in a few large roasting tins and roast in the oven for 30 minutes until well browned. Add all the bones to the stockpot or pan along with the vegetables.

Pour the fat out of the roasting tins into a saucepan, add 1 litre of the reserved water, place over high heat and bring to a simmer, stirring with a wooden spoon to loosen any coagulated juices. Add this liquid to the bones and vegetables. Add additional reserved water, if necessary, to just cover the bones; the liquid should come no higher than 2 cm below the rim of the pan, as the volume will expand slightly during cooking.

Bring the broth to the boil, skimming off the scum that rises to the top. Reduce the heat to low and add the thyme, bay leaves, peppercorns and garlic. Simmer for 24–32 hours. Just before finishing, add the parsley and simmer for another 10 minutes. Strain the broth into a large container. Cover and cool in the refrigerator. Remove the congealed fat that rises to the top. Transfer the bone broth to smaller airtight containers and place in the fridge or, for long-term storage, the freezer. The broth can be stored in the fridge for 3–4 days or frozen for up to 3 months.

MAKES 3.5–4 LITRES

ENDNOTES

1. Selection for smaller brains in Holocene human evolution. Human Biology 1988;60:395–405.
2. A 2011 peer-reviewed article had this to say when it comes to an overall paleo approach to health: 'It is increasingly recognised that certain fundamental changes in diet and lifestyle that occurred after the Neolithic Revolution, and especially after the Industrial Revolution and the Modern Age, are too recent, on an evolutionary time scale, for the human genome to have completely adapted. This mismatch between our ancient physiology and the Western diet and lifestyle underlies many so-called diseases of civilization, including coronary heart disease, obesity, hypertension, type 2 diabetes, epithelial cell cancers, autoimmune disease, and osteoporosis, which are rare or virtually absent in hunter–gatherers and other non-Westernised populations. It is therefore proposed that the adoption of diet and lifestyle that mimic the beneficial characteristics of the pre-agricultural environment is an effective strategy to reduce the risk of chronic degenerative diseases'. Carrera-Bastos P, Fontes-Villalba M, O'Keefe JH, et al. The western diet and lifestyle and diseases of civilization. Research Reports in Clinical Cardiology, 8 March 2011.
3. Max Planck researcher, Dr Michael Richards' publications: http://www.eva.mpg.de/evolution/staff/richards/publications.htm.
4. Katzenberg MA. Stable isotope analysis: a tool for studying past diet, demography, and life history. In Katzenberg MA, Saunders SR, eds. Biological Anthropology of the Human Skeleton. 2nd edn. Hoboken: Wiley-Liss, 2008:413–41.
5. Schoeninger MJ, DeNiro M. Nitrogen and carbon isotopic composition of bone collagen from marine and terrestrial animals. Geochimica et Cosmochimica Acta 1984;48:635–9.
6. Schoeninger MJ. Stable isotope studies in human evolution. Evolutionary Anthropology 1995;4(3):83–98.
7. van der Merwe, NJ. Carbon isotopes, photosynthesis, and archeology. American Scientist 1982;70:596–606.
8. US News & World Report.
9. http://www.humanholistics.com/who-we-see/gluten-sensitivity-and-celiac-disease.
10. Hasselbalch SG, et al. Changes in cerebral blood flow and carbohydrate metabolism during acute hyperketonemia. Am J Physiol 1996;270:E746–51.
11. We have been told this myth for so long now – but it was never true. According to Dr Richard Feinman, Professor of Biochemistry at Downstate Medical Center (SUNY) in New York, 'The deleterious effects of fat have been measured in the presence of high carbohydrate. A high fat diet in the presence of high carbohydrate is different than a high fat diet in the presence of low carbohydrate'.
12. Cahill GF Jr, Veech RL. Ketoacids? Good medicine? Trans Am Clin Climatol Assoc. 2003;114:149–61; discussion 162–3. http://www.ncbi.nlm.nih.gov/pubmed/12813917.
13. Malhotra A. Saturated fats not the major issue. BMJ 2013;347:f6340. DOI: 10.1136/bmj.f6340.
14. Santos FL, et al. Systematic review and meta-analysis of clinical trials of the effects of low carbohydrate diets on cardiovascular risk factors. Obesity Reviews. Epub 21 August 2012.
15. Burns CM, Chen K, Kaszniak AW, et al. Higher serum glucose levels are associated with cerebral hypometabolism in Alzheimer regions. Neurology, 23 April 2013;80(17):1557–64. DOI: 10.1212/WNL.0b013e31828f17de. Epub 27 March 2013.
16. Crane PK, Walker R, Hubbard RA, et al. Glucose levels and risk of dementia. N Engl J Med 8 August 2013;369:540–8. DOI: 10.1056/NEJMoa1215740.
17. Lead researcher Cynthia Kenyon stated in her conclusions: 'We found that adding a small amount of glucose to the medium (0.1-2 per cent) shortened the lifespan of C. elegans … Together these findings raise the possibility that a low-sugar diet might have beneficial effects on lifespan in higher organisms'. Lee SJ, Murphy CT, and Kenyon C. Glucose shortens the lifespan of Caenorhabditis elegans by down-regulating aquaporin gene expression. Cell Metab November 2009;10(5):379–91.
18. The conclusions stated: 'This retrospective analysis of patients from a private clinic adhering to a high-fat, low carbohydrate, adequate protein diet demonstrated reductions in critical metabolic mediators including insulin, leptin, glucose, triglycerides, and free T3 … Patients in this study demonstrated a similar directional impact on the measured parameters when compared to studies using more established models of longevity such as caloric restriction'. Rosedale R, Westman EC, Konhilas JP. Clinical experience of a diet designed to reduce aging. Journal of Applied Research 2009;9(4).
19. Veech RL. The therapeutic implications of ketone bodies: the effects of ketone bodies in pathological conditions: ketosis, ketogenic diet, redox states, insulin resistance, and mitochondrial metabolism. Prostaglandins Leukot Essent Fatty Acids March 2004;70(3):309–19.
20. Spreadbury I. Comparison with ancestral diets suggests dense acellular carbohydrates promote an inflammatory microbiota, and may be the primary dietary cause of leptin resistance and obesity. Diabetes, Metabolic Syndrome and Obesity: Targets and Therapy. 4 July 2012.
21. Lecoultre V, Ravussin E, Redman, LM. The fall in leptin concentration is a major determinant of the metabolic adaptation induced by caloric restriction independently of the changes in leptin circadian rhythms. The Journal of Clin Endocrinology & Metabolism 1 September 2011:96(9).
22. Lozupone CA, Li M, Campbell TB, et al. Alterations in the gut microbiota associated with hiv-1 infection. Cell Host & Microbe 11 September 2013:14(3):329–39.

23. Scher JU, Sczesnak A, Longman RS. Expansion of intestinal Prevotella copri correlates with enhanced susceptibility to arthritis. eLife November 2013;2:e01202, http://dx.doi.org/10.7554/eLife.01202.

24. Pusztai A, et al. The toxicity of Phaseolus vulgaris lectins: Nitrogen balance and immunochemical studies. J Sci Food Agric 1981; 32:1037–46.

25. To quote Sayer Ji, brilliant researcher and founder of GreenMedInfo: 'One must also account for the "invisible thorn", which is wheat lectin – known more technically as *Wheat Germ Agglutinin* (WGA) – and which can cause a broad range of adverse health effects, even while being undetected through conventional screenings' and 'What is unique about WGA is that it can do *direct* damage to the majority of tissues in the human body without requiring a specific set of genetic susceptibilities and/or immune-mediated articulations. This may explain why chronic inflammatory and degenerative conditions are endemic to wheat-consuming populations even when overt allergies or intolerances to wheat gluten appear exceedingly rare'. http://www.greenmedinfo.com/page/opening-pandoras-bread-box-critical-role-wheat-lectin-human-disease.

26. http://www.glutenfreeandmore.com/issues/4_15/qa_augsep11-2554-1.html

27. Ludvigsson JF, Montgomery SM, Ekbom A, Brandt L, Granath F. Small-intestinal histopathology and mortality risk in celiac disease. Journal of the American Medical Association September 2009;16;302(11):1171–8.

28. Hadjivassiliou M, Sanders DA, Grunewald RA, Woodroofe N, Boscolo S and Aeschlimann D. Gluten sensitivity: from gut to brain. Lancet Neurol 2010;9:318–30

29. According to Dr Fasano, discoverer of zonulin and the mechanisms of its action: 'Dysregulation of this conceptual zonulin model may contribute to disease states that involve disordered intercellular communication, including developmental and intestinal disorders leading to autoimmune disease (that is, CD and type 1 diabetes), tissue inflammation, malignant transformation, and metastasis.' Fasano A. Intestinal zonulin: open sesame! Gut 2001; 49:159–62. DOI:10.1136/gut.49.2.159.

30. A recent peer-reviewed article in *Diabetes, Metabolic Syndrome and Obesity: Targets and Therapy* (titled 'Comparison with ancestral diets suggests dense acellular carbohydrates promote an inflammatory microbiota, and may be the primary dietary cause of leptin resistance and obesity') stated in its conclusions: 'We should not settle for the meager improvements attainable from the consensus dietary advice when it is already clear that so much more might be achieved. Our sights should be set high; to see how close we can move levels of industrialized metabolic health toward those enjoyed by non-Westernized populations. While many will resist making dietary changes of such magnitude, official advice must nonetheless point in the correct direction, allowing individuals to make informed decisions … A dietary pattern with carbohydrates exclusively from cellular low-density sources may remove the root cause of a range of our most prevalent diseases. The potential savings in health-care costs should be borne in mind, and the hypothesis tested.'

    Spreadbury I. Comparison with ancestral diets suggests dense acellular carbohydrates promote an inflammatory microbiota, and may be the primary dietary cause of leptin resistance and obesity. Diabetes, Metabolic Syndrome and Obesity: Targets and Therapy July 2012;2012:5: 175–189. http://dx.doi.org/10.2147/DMSO.S33473_

31. Liener IE. Implications of antinutritional components in soybean foods. Crit Rev Food Sci Nutr 1994; 34:31–67.

32. Gupta YP. Antinutritional and toxic factors in food legumes: a review. Plant Foods Hum Nutr 1987; 37:201–28.

33. FAO/WHO Expert Consultation. Protein Quality Evaluation. Food and Agricultural Organization of the United Nations, FAO Food and Nutrition Paper 51, Rome, 1991.

34. Nutritionist Pro Dietary Software. http://www.nutritionistpro.com/

35. Gilani GS, Cockell KA, Sepehr E. Effects of antinutritional factors on protein digestibility and amino acid availability in foods. J AOAC Int May–June 2005;88(3):967–87.

36. Hughes JS, Acevedo E, Bressani R, et al. Effects of dietary fiber and tannins on protein utilization in dry beans (Phaseolus vulgaris). Food Res Int 1996;29:331–8.

37. Hallberg L, Hulthén L. Prediction of dietary iron absorption: an algorithm for calculating absorption and bioavailability of dietary iron. The American Journal of Clinical Nutrition May 2000;71(5):1147–60.

38. Gibson RS, Bailey KB, Gibbs M, Ferguson EL. A review of phytate, iron, zinc, and calcium concentrations in plant-based complementary foods used in low-income countries and implications for bioavailability. Food Nutr Bull June 2010;31(2 suppl.):S134–46.

39. Couzy F, Mansourian R, Labate A, Guinchard S, Montagne DH, Dirren H. Effect of dietary phytic acid on zinc absorption in the healthy elderly, as assessed by serum concentration curve tests. Br J Nutr Aug 1998;80(2):177–82.

40. Sandberg AS. Bioavailability of minerals in legumes. Br J Nutr Dec 2002;88 (3 suppl.):S281–5.

41. Pusztai A, Greer F, Grant G. Specific uptake of dietary lectins into the systemic circulation of rats. Biochemical Society Transactions 1989;17, 527–8.

42. Pusztai A, Ewen SWB, Grant G, et al. Plant (food) lectins as signal molecules: Effects on the morphology and bacterial ecology of the small intestine. In: Kilpatrick DC, Van Driessche E, Bog-Hansen TC, eds. Lectin Reviews. St. Louis: Sigma, 1991;I:1–15.

43. Greer F, Pusztai A. Toxicity of kidney bean (Phaseolus vulgaris) in rats: changes in intestinal permeability. Digestion 1985;32:42–46.

44. Pusztai A, Ewen SW, Grant G, et al. Antinutritive effects of wheat-germ agglutinin and other N-acetylglucosamine-specific lectins. Br J Nutr July 1993;70(1):313–21.

45. Wang Q, Yu LG, Campbell BJ, Milton JD, Rhodes JM. Identification of intact peanut lectin in peripheral venous blood. Lancet 1998;352:1831–2.
46. Caron M, Steve AP. Lectins and Pathology. London: Taylor & Francis, 2000.
47. Liener IE. Nutritional significance of lectins in the diet. In: Liener IE, Sharon N, Goldstein IJ, eds. The Lectins: Properties, Functions, and Applications in Biology and Medicine: Orlando: Academic Press, 1986:527–52.
48. Pusztai A. Dietary lectins are metabolic signals for the gut and modulate immune and hormone functions. Eur J Clin Nutr 1993b; 47: 691–9.
49. Schechter Y. Bound lectins that mimic insulin produce persistent insulin-like activities. Endocrinology 1983;113:1921–6.
50. Chrispeels MJ, Raikel NV. Lectins, lectin genes, and their role in plant defense. Plant Cell 1991; 3:1–9.
51. Boufassa C, Lafont J, Rouanet JM, Besancon P. Thermal inactivation of lectins (PHA) isolated from Phaseolus vulgaris. Food Chem 1986 ;20: 295–304.
52. Grant G, More LJ, McKenzie NH, Pusztai A. The effect of heating on the haemagglutinating activity and nutritional properties of bean (Phaseolus vulgaris) seeds. J Sci Food Agric 1982;33:1324–6.
53. Pusztai A, Grant G. Assessment of lectin inactivation by heat and digestion. In: Methods in Molecular Medicine: Vol. 9: Lectin methods and protocols. Rhodes JM, Milton JD, eds. Totowa, NJ: Humana Press Inc. 1998.
54. Hallberg L, Hulthén L. Prediction of dietary iron absorption: an algorithm for calculating absorption and bioavailability of dietary iron. Am J Clin Nutr May 2000;71(5):1147–60.
55. Hurrell RF, Juillerat MA, Reddy MB, Lynch SR, Dassenko SA, Cook JD. Soy protein, phytate, and iron absorption in humans. Am J Clin Nutr Sept 1992; 56(3): 573–8.
56. Couzy F, Mansourian R, Labate A, Guinchard S, Montagne DH, Dirren H. Effect of dietary phytic acid on zinc absorption in the healthy elderly, as assessed by serum concentration curve tests. Br J Nutr Aug 1998; 80(2):177–82.
57. Gibson RS, Bailey KB, Gibbs M, Ferguson EL. A review of phytate, iron, zinc, and calcium concentrations in plant-based complementary foods used in low-income countries and implications for bioavailability. Food Nutr Bull June 2010; 31(2 suppl.):S134–46.
58. Sandberg AS. Bioavailability of minerals in legumes. Br J Nutr Dec 2002;88(3 suppl.):S281–5.
59. Gilani GS, Cockell KA, Sepehr E. Effects of antinutritional factors on protein digestibility and amino acid availability in foods. J AOAC Int. May–June 2005;88(3):967–87.
60. Grant G. Anti-nutritional effects of soyabean: a review. Prog Food Nutr Sci 1989;13(3–4):317–48.
61. Losso JN. The biochemical and functional food properties of the bowman-birk inhibitor. Crit Rev Food Sci Nutr Jan 2008;48(1): 94–118.
62. Pirke KM, Schweiger U, Laessle R, Dickhaut B, Schweiger M, Waechtler M. Dieting influences the menstrual cycle: vegetarian versus nonvegetarian diet. Fertil Steril Dec 1986;46(6):1083–90.
63. Román GC. Autism: transient in utero hypothyroxinemia related to maternal flavonoid ingestion during pregnancy and to other environmental antithyroid agents. J Neurol Sci Nov 2007; 262(1–2):15–26.
64. Alvarez JR, Torres-Pinedo R. Interactions of soybean lectin, soyasaponins, and glycinin with rabbit jejunal mucosa in vitro. Pediatr Res Sep 1982;16(9):728–31.
65. Baumann E, Stoya G, Völkner A, Richter W, Lemke C, Linss W. Hemolysis of human erythrocytes with saponin affects the membrane structure. Acta Histochem Feb 2000;102(1):21–35.
66. Francis G, Kerem Z, Makkar HP, Becker K. The biological action of saponins in animal systems: a review. Br J Nutr Dec 2002;88(6):587–605.
67. Gee JM, Johnson IT. Interactions between hemolytic saponins, bile salts and small intestinal mucosa in the rat. J Nutr Nov 1988;118(11):1391–7.
68. Gee JM, Wal JM, Miller K, et al. Effect of saponin on the transmucosal passage of beta-lactoglobulin across the proximal small intestine of normal and beta-lactoglobulin-sensitized rats. Toxicology 28 February 1997;117(2–3):219–28.
69. Johnson IT, Gee JM, Price K, Curl C, Fenwick GR. Influence of saponins on gut permeability and active nutrient transport in vitro. J Nutr Nov 1986;116(11):2270–7.
70. Among the best is Daniel, KT. *The Whole Soy Story*. I also devote an entire chapter to outlining the dangers of this noxious and health-compromising member of the legume family in my book *Primal Body, Primal Mind*.
71. Gresham GA, et al. The independent production of atherosclerosis and thrombosis in the rat. Br J Exp Pathol 1960;41:395–402.
72. Boyle EM, et al. Atherosclerosis. Ann Thorac Surg 1997;64:S47–56.
73. Kritchevsky D, et al. Influence of native and randomized peanut oil on lipid metabolism and aortic sudanophilia in the vervet monkey. Atherosclerosis 1982;42:53–58.
74. Kritchevsky D, Tepper SA, Klurfeld DM. Lectin may contribute to the atherogenicity of peanut oil. Lipids Aug 1998;33(8):821–3.
75. Conn EE. Cyanogenic glycosides. In: Bell AE; Charlwood BV, eds. Encyclopedia of Plant Physiology. Secondary plant products 1980;8:461–92.
76. Noah ND, et al. Food poisoning from raw red kidney beans. Brit Med J 1980; 2: 236–7.
77. Rodhouse JC, Haugh CA, Roberts D, Gilbert RJ. Red kidney bean poisoning in the UK: an analysis of 50 suspected incidents between 1976 and 1989. Epidemiol Infect Dec 1990;105(3):485–91.

78. Tuxen MK, Nielsen HV, Birgens H. Poisoning by kidney beans (Phaseolus vulgaris). Ugeskr Laeger 16 December 1991;153(51):3628–9.

79. Red kidney beans been banned from importation to South Africa due to 'their potential toxicity to humans'. Venter FS, Thiel PG. Red kidney beans–to eat or not to eat? S Afr Med J Apr 1995;85(4):250–2.

80. Elias PK, et al. Serum cholesterol and cognitive performance in the Framingham Heart Study. Psychosomatic medicine 2005;67(1): 24–30.

81. The Organic Center, AAAS Session 2009. Living Soil, Food Quality and the Future of Food, February 2009.

82. Newhope360.com 27 February 2009.

83. New Evidence Confirms the Nutritional Superiority of Plant-Based Organic Foods. www.organic-center.org/reportfiles/5367_Nutrient_Content_SSR_FINAL_V2.pdf.

84. Organic Retailers and Growers Association of Australia, 2000, as cited in *Pesticides and You*, Spring 2000;20(1). News from Beyond Pesticides/National Coalition Against the Misuse of Pesticides.

85. Wang SY, Lin HS. Compost as a soil supplement increases the level of antioxidant compounds and oxygen radical absorbance capacity in strawberries. J Agric Food Chem 5 November 2003;51(23):6844–50.

86. Carbonaro M, Mattera M, Nicoli S, Bergamo P, Cappelloni M. Modulation of antioxidant compounds in organic vs conventional fruit (peach, Prunus persica L., and pear, Pyrus communis L.). J Agric Food Chem 11 September 2002;50(19):5458–62.

87. Asami DK, Hong YJ, Barrett DM, Mitchell AE. Comparison of the total phenolic and ascorbic acid content of freeze-dried and air-dried marionberry, strawberry, and corn grown using conventional, organic, and sustainable agricultural practices. J Agric Food Chem 26 February 2003;51(5):1237–41.

88. Lombardi-Boccia G, Lucarini M, Lanzi S, Aguzzi A, Cappelloni M. Nutrients and antioxidant molecules in yellow plums (Prunus domestica L.) from conventional and organic productions: a comparative study. J Agric Food Chem 14 January 2004;52(1):90–4.

89. Häkkinen SH, Törrönen AR. Content of flavonols and selected phenolic acids in strawberries and Vaccinium species: influence of cultivar, cultivation site and technique. Food Res Int. 2000;33(6):517–24.

90. Davis DR, Epp MD, Riordan HD. Changes in USDA food composition data for 43 garden crops, 1950 to 1999. J Am Coll Nutr Dec 2004;23(6):669–82.

91. Siriwoharn T, Wrolstad RE, Finn CE, Pereira CB. Influence of cultivar, maturity, and sampling on blackberry (Rubus L. Hybrids) anthocyanins, polyphenolics, and antioxidant properties. J Agric Food Chem 29 December 2004;52(26):8021–30.

92. Yoo KM, Lee KW, Park JB, Lee HJ, Hwang IK. Variation in major antioxidants and total antioxidant activity of yuzu (Citrus junos Sieb ex Tanaka) during maturation and between cultivars. J Agric Food Chem 22 September 2004;52(19):5907–13.

93. Serrano M, Guillen F, Martinez-Romero D, Castillo S, Valero D. Chemical constituents and antioxidant activity of sweet cherry at different ripening stages. J Agric Food Chem 6 April 2005;53(7):2741–5.

94. Moure A, Cruz JM, Franco D, et al. Review: natural antioxidants from residual sources. Food Chem 2001;72:145–71.

95. Giuntini D, Graziani G, Lercari B, et al. Changes in carotenoid and ascorbic acid contents in fruits of different tomato genotypes related to the depletion of UV-B radiation. J Agric Food Chem 20 April 2005;53(8):3174–81.

96. Diaz dlG, Quinlivan EP, Klaus SM, et al. Folate biofortification in tomatoes by engineering the pteridine branch of folate synthesis. Proc Natl Acad Sci USA 21 September 2004;101(38):13720–5.

97. Rapisarda P, Clabretta ML, Romano G, Intrigliolo F. Nitrogen metabolism components as a tool to discriminate between organic and conventional citrus fruits. J Agric Food Chem 6 April 2005;53(7):2664–9.

98. Bouchard MF, Bellinger DC, Wright RO, Weisskopf MG. Attention-Deficit/Hyperactivity Disorder and Urinary Metabolites of Organophosphate Pesticides. Pediatrics May 2010. DOI: 10.1542/peds.2009–3058.

99. Cynthia L Curl, Richard A Fenske and Kai Elgethun wrote: 'Dose estimates suggest that consumption of organic fruits, vegetables, and juice can reduce children's exposure levels from above to below the US Environmental Protection Agency's current guidelines, thereby shifting exposures from a range of uncertain risk to a range of negligible risk,' adding, 'Consumption of organic produce appears to provide a relatively simple way for parents to reduce their children's exposure to OP pesticides'.

    Curl CL, Fenske RA, Elgethun K. Organophosphorus pesticide exposure of urban and suburban pre-school children with organic and conventional diets. *Environmental Health Perspectives.* ehponline.org posted online 31 October 2002.

100. Original study: Lu C, Knutson DE, Fisker-Andersen J, Fenske RA. Biological Monitoring Survey of Organophosphorus Pesticide Exposure among Preschool Children in the Seattle Metropolitan area. *Environmental Health Perspectives* March 2001;109(3):299–303. Subsequent study: Curl CL, Fenske RA, Elgethun K. Organophosphorus pesticide exposure of urban and suburban pre-school children with organic and conventional diets. *Environmental Health Perspectives.* ehponline.org posted online 31 October 2002.

101. The study was conducted by The Institute of Food Safety and Nutrition under The Danish Veterinary and Food Administration, The Department of Human Nutrition and Centre for Advanced Food Studies under The Royal Veterinary and Agricultural University, and Riso National Laboratory. *Journal of Agricultural and Food Chemistry* 2003; 51(19):5671–6.

102. http://www.qlif.org/.

THANK YOU

Pete

- Once again thank you to my beautiful partner in life and love, Nicola. I am seriously the luckiest bloke on the planet. Thank you for nurturing me and the little bunnies, Indii and Chilli, with love and food. I love you!
- To my bunnies, Indii and Chilli – you know this book wouldn't have come about if it weren't for you. I love you both so much and you are both so unique in your own special ways. I hope that by the time your own children are at school this way of living will be considered normal and the current dietary guidelines considered extreme.
- Nora Gedgaudas and Lisa Collins, it goes without saying that you are our family now and Nic and I love you both so much!
- Mark Roper (photography) and Deb Kaloper (styling) – thanks for once again making my food shine brightly!
- To Steve Brown (photography) and Trish Heagerty (styling) – thanks for creating some great lifestyle images.
- To Mary Small, the coolest book publisher in the Southern Hemisphere – keep on standing out from the pack and delivering books that will help change the world.
- To Jane Winning – thanks once again for making sure all my recipes are tested for everyone cooking from the book.
- To Megan Johnston – thank you for your careful and thorough editing.
- To Kirby Armstrong – thanks again for creating a fabulous design for the book.
- To Monica and Jacinta Cannataci – girls, I can't thank you enough and I am so happy that you have discovered that food really is medicine. You are the doctors of the future.
- To Charlotte Ree – thanks for being the best publicist any author could wish to work with.
- To Mum – thanks for passing on your love of cooking.
- And finally to my mentors and the trailblazers in health and nutrition, I couldn't have done it without you: Trevor Hendy, Luke Hines, Helen Padarin, Pete Melov, Rudy Eckhardt, Pete Bablis, William (Bill) Davis, Tim Noakes, Gary Fettke, David Perlmutter, Gary Taubes, Frank Lipman, Wes and Charlotte Carr, Nahko Bear, Michael Franti, Trevor Hall, David Gillespie, Ben Balzer, Loren Cordain, Bruce Fife, Mat Lalonde, Martha Herbert, Joseph Mercola, Sally Fallon, Dr Natasha Campbell-McBride, Kitsa Yanniotis and Donna Gates.

Nora

Sharing what I have come to know about this topic has been a considerable source of passion for me. It is such an honour to do so. It is my deepest hope that what is written in this book becomes more than words to those who read it, that it will be used as a practical guide for restoring health and awakening fresh thinking, awareness and a new perspective. Coming to what I know has been a long process of researching and learning from similarly passionate and highly diverse mentors, together with the writings of numerous pioneers and world class researchers along the way. I want to sincerely thank the visionaries at the Ancestral Health Society who have sought to bring the ideas and people from the broader field of evolutionary nutrition together, allowing us to better learn from one another.

I am more than grateful to Pete Evans and Nicola Robinson for being true friends and champions of me and my work, as well as real, foundational health for all.

Some key mentors/friends I would like to thank include Datis Kharrazian, Aristo Vojdani, Ron Rosedale, Tom O'Bryan, Colleen Dunseth, Siegfried Othmer, Sue Othmer, Mary Enig and Janet Lang. Authors whose works have served to inspire me (apart from the aforementioned) include George Cahill, Richard Veech, Richard Feinman, Stephen Phinney, Peter Attia, Gary Taubes, Jeff Volek, John Briffa, Andreas Einfeldt and Collin Champ.

I also want to thank Jay Wortman for his excellent research, his dedication to First Nation peoples and his passionate and compassionate devotion to the education and health of others. And how could I forget my buddy, Jimmy Moore, for his tireless and rare dedication to valuable, civilised and rational discourse? I am also eternally grateful for the works of Weston A. Price, Francis Pottenger and Vilhjálmur Stefánsson. And if I have forgotten anyone living and breathing here I sincerely apologise.

Last but certainly not least, I am forever in debt to Lisa Collins for the pillar of strength, support and love she has allowed me to lean on these many years.

INDEX

D

E

F

T

Z

A PLUM BOOK

First published in 2015 by
Pan Macmillan Australia Pty Limited
Level 25, 1 Market Street,
Sydney, NSW 2000, Australia

Level 1, 15–19 Claremont Street,
South Yarra, Victoria 3141, Australia

Design by Kirby Armstrong
Photography by Mark Roper and Steve Brown
Prop and food styling by Deb Kaloper and Trish Heagerty
Food preparation by Monica Cannataci and Jacinta Cannataci
Edited by Megan Johnston
Typeset by Pauline Haas
Index by Jo Rudd
Colour reproduction by Splitting Image Colour Studio
Printed and bound in China by 1010 Printing International Limited

Recipe for Paleo Parfait with Coconut Cream (page 101) adapted with permission from *Clean Living* by Luke Hines and Scott Gooding, 2013, published by Hachette Australia.

A CIP catalogue record for this book is available from the National Library of Australia.

10 9 8 7 6 5 4 3 2

IMPORTANT NOTE TO READERS
The information provided in this publication aims to give general guidance relating to the subject matter and does not purport to be comprehensive. You should carefully evaluate the accuracy, completeness and relevance of this information to your purposes and health particularities. We do not give any warranty that the information is free from error or suitable for your purposes. It is not intended as a substitute for specialist advice in individual circumstances, and no responsibility is accepted for any loss arising from reliance on it.

If you are pregnant or have any particular health condition, we strongly advise that you consult a qualified health and medical practitioner prior to making any changes to your diet or lifestyle and have them monitor your progress at all times. Although we in good faith believe that the information provided will help you live a healthier life, relying on the information contained in this publication may not give you the results you desire or may cause negative health consequences. For this reason we recommend you always consult a medical health professional before making any changes to your diet or lifestyle.